HEBREW
THROUGH
PRAYER

דֶּרֶךְ תְּפִלָּה

1

Terry Kaye

Karen Trager

Patrice Goldstein Mason

BEHRMAN HOUSE, INC.

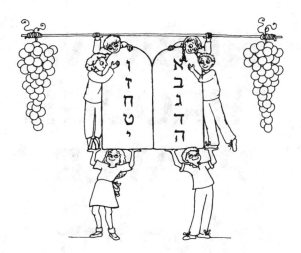

The editor and publisher gratefully acknowledge the cooperation of the following
sources of photographs for this book:
Bill Aron, 19, 20; Francene Keery, cover, 4, 6, 23, 31, 36, 41, 42, 64, 66, 69, 74, 76, 84.

Special thanks to Congregation Emanu-El of the city of New York for their cooperation
(photographs appear on pages 6, 23, 41, 42, 64, 66, 69, 74).

Special thanks to the Society for the Advancement of Judaism for their cooperation
(photographs appear on cover and pages 4, 31, 36, 76, 84).

Special thanks to the Solomon Schechter of Greater Boston, Linda Silverstein,
and the Weber family for the photo on page 78.

Book Design: Itzhack Shelomi
Cover Design: Robert J. O'Dell
Illustrator: Jana Ben-Moshe
Project Editor: Adam Siegel

Contents

1   בָּרְכוּ

A hundred years ago, when the Jews lived in little villages in Eastern Europe called *shtetls*, the synagogue *klapper* ("knocker") went from house to house knocking on the shutters when it was time to come to the synagogue to pray.

Today, although no one comes to our homes to call us to pray, the leader of the service announces the official beginning of the prayer service with the בָּרְכוּ, the Call to Prayer.

• • • • • • • • •

Practice reading the בָּרְכוּ aloud.

1   בָּרְכוּ אֶת־יְיָ הַמְבֹרָךְ.

    Praise Adonai, who is to be praised.

2   בָּרוּךְ יְיָ הַמְבֹרָךְ לְעוֹלָם וָעֶד.

    Praised is Adonai, who is praised forever and ever.

4

Search and Circle

Circle the Hebrew word(s) that means the same as the English.

English			
forever and ever	אֶת	לְעוֹלָם וָעֶד	בָּרְכוּ
Adonai	יְיָ	בָּרְכוּ	בָּרוּךְ
praise	אֶת	הַמְבֹרָךְ	בָּרְכוּ
who is praised	הַמְבֹרָךְ	לְעוֹלָם וָעֶד	אֶת

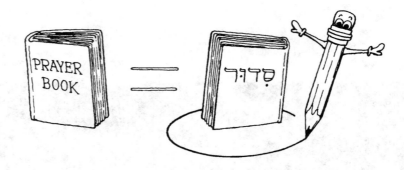

Match Game

Connect the Hebrew word(s) to its English meaning.

English	Hebrew
who is praised	בָּרְכוּ
Adonai	יְיָ
praise	הַמְבֹרָךְ
forever and ever	בָּרוּךְ
praised	לְעוֹלָם וָעֶד

Prayer Dictionary (side column)

בָּרְכוּ
praise

אֶת
(no English meaning)

יְיָ
Adonai

הַמְבֹרָךְ
who is praised

בָּרוּךְ
praised, blessed

לְעוֹלָם וָעֶד
forever and ever

What's Missing?

Complete each prayer phrase with the the missing Hebrew word(s).

אֶת יְיָ הַמְבֹרָךְ. _____ praise

בָּרוּךְ יְיָ הַמְבֹרָךְ _____ _____ forever and ever

בָּרְכוּ אֶת _____ הַמְבֹרָךְ. Adonai

יְיָ הַמְבֹרָךְ לְעוֹלָם וָעֶד. _____ praised

• • • • • • • • •

6

In the Synagogue

How did the בָּרְכוּ get its name? בָּרְכוּ is the first word of the prayer. The first word of a Hebrew prayer is often the name by which the prayer is known.

The בָּרְכוּ is thousands of years old. The Jewish people have said the בָּרְכוּ since the time of the Temple — בֵּית הַמִּקְדָשׁ. Today, the leader of the service calls us to pray with the very same words that were recited in the Temple.

The cantor or rabbi chants

בָּרְכוּ אֶת־יְיָ הַמְבֹרָךְ.

and the congregation answers

בָּרוּךְ יְיָ הַמְבֹרָךְ לְעוֹלָם וָעֶד.

Just as we respond to a friendly "hello" with a greeting, we answer the Call to Prayer with the response that, yes, we will pray.

True or False

Put a ✔ next to each sentence that is *true*.

_____ The בָּרְכוּ is the Call to Prayer.

_____ A Hebrew prayer gets its name from the last word of the prayer.

_____ The בָּרְכוּ marks the start of the main part of the service.

_____ The בָּרְכוּ is a new prayer.

_____ The בָּרְכוּ tells us to praise God.

Discover the Prayer

Cross out every other letter in the design. Then read the prayer.

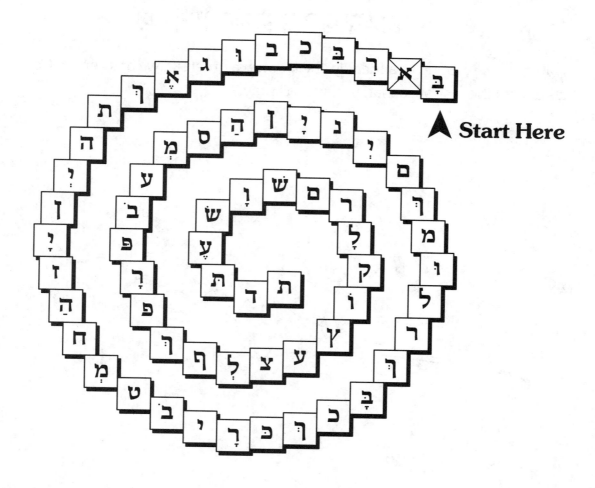

▲ Start Here

8

Family Letters

The words below contain family letters: כ כך and בב. Practice reading them.

כְּמוֹךְ	יָדְךָ	תּוֹכֵנוּ	לָךְ	לְךָ	כָּל	מֶלֶךְ	1	כך
מְכַלְכֵּל	כְּמַלְכֵּנוּ	כָּמֹכָה	מִכָּל	אָכַל	כָּל	2		ככ
אֲבָל	כּוֹכָבִים	בִּדְבָרוֹ	בַּלֵּבָב	מַכַּבִּי	בְּבֵית	3		בב

Roots

Three words in the בָּרְכוּ look and sound similar:

בָּרוּךְ   הַמְבֹרָךְ   בָּרְכוּ

Which three letters appear in each word? _____ _____ _____
(Hint: כ כך and בב are family letters.)

Most Hebrew words are built on roots.
A root usually consists of three letters.
A root has no vowels.

The three words above share the root ברכ (or ברך).
The root ברכ means "bless" or "praise."

Circle the three root letters in each of these words:

הַמְבֹרָךְ   בָּרְכוּ   בָּרוּךְ

Write the root. _____ _____ _____

Did You Know?

The בָּרְכוּ is also part of the blessing said before we read from the Torah.

• • • • • • • • •

Practice reading the Torah blessing.

1 בָּרְכוּ אֶת־יְיָ הַמְבֹרָךְ.

2 בָּרוּךְ יְיָ הַמְבֹרָךְ לְעוֹלָם וָעֶד.

3 בָּרוּךְ אַתָּה, יְיָ אֱלֹהֵינוּ, מֶלֶךְ הָעוֹלָם,

4 אֲשֶׁר בָּחַר בָּנוּ מִכָּל הָעַמִּים, וְנָתַן לָנוּ אֶת תּוֹרָתוֹ.

5 בָּרוּךְ אַתָּה, יְיָ, נוֹתֵן הַתּוֹרָה.

Why do you think the בָּרְכוּ was made a part of the Torah blessing?

_____

_____

_____

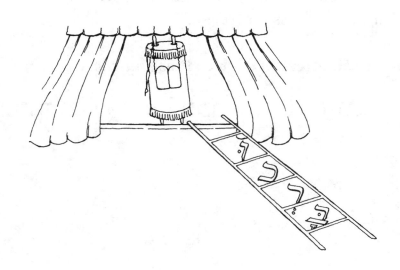

10

God's Name

God's name is mysterious. A long time ago, the Kohanim, the Priests who served in the Temple in Jerusalem, knew how to pronounce God's name. But they kept it a secret. The High Priest would say God's name only once a year — on Yom Kippur. Today we are not really sure how God's name was pronounced, so we say Adonai.

We pronounce God's name יְיָ as אֲדוֹנָי.
God's name is written in many different ways.
In the בָּרְכוּ God's name is written יְיָ.
In other places in the סִדּוּר, and in the Bible (תַּנַ"ךְ), you may see God's name written יְהוָֹה. יְהוָֹה is also pronounced Adonai.
In other Hebrew books you may see God's name written like this: ה׳.

• • • • • • • • •

Write *three* ways that God's name may be written.

_____ _____ _____

How do you pronounce all these words?
You will learn other names for God in later lessons.

Reading Practice

Practice reading the following sentences. Circle God's name wherever it appears.

1 בָּרְכוּ אֶת־יְיָ הַמְבֹרָךְ.

2 בָּרוּךְ יְיָ הַמְבֹרָךְ לְעוֹלָם וָעֶד.

3 מֵאֵין כָּמוֹךְ, יְהוָֹה, גָּדוֹל אַתָּה וְגָדוֹל שִׁמְךָ בִּגְבוּרָה.

4 כִּי לְךָ ה׳ הַגְּדֻלָּה וְהַגְּבוּרָה וְהַתִּפְאֶרֶת.

5 יְיָ צְבָאוֹת שְׁמוֹ.

6 גָּדוֹל ה׳ וּמְהֻלָּל מְאֹד, וְלִגְדֻלָּתוֹ אֵין חֵקֶר.

11

How Would You Respond?

In the בָּרְכוּ the cantor or rabbi *calls* us to pray. We *hear* and we *answer*, "yes" we will pray.

● ● ● ● ● ● ● ● ●

In each example below, tell how you would respond.

You Hear:	You Do or Say:
The doorbell ringing	_____
Mom calling	_____
A neighbor carrying heavy packages	_____
Latkes sizzling in oil	_____
The alarm clock buzzing	_____
Haman's name	_____
בָּרְכוּ אֶת־יְיָ הַמְבֹרָךְ	_____

12

Fluent Reading

Each phrase contains a word you know. Practice reading the lines below.

• • • • • • • • •

1 בָּרְכוּ אֶת־יְיָ הַמְבֹרָךְ.

2 בָּרוּךְ יְיָ הַמְבֹרָךְ לְעוֹלָם וָעֶד.

3 בָּרוּךְ אַתָּה יְיָ הָאֵל הַקָּדוֹשׁ.

4 יְיָ עֹז לְעַמּוֹ יִתֵּן, יְיָ יְבָרֵךְ אֶת עַמּוֹ בַשָּׁלוֹם.

5 כִּי יָדַעְתִּי אֶת אֲשֶׁר תְּבָרֵךְ מְבֹרָךְ, וַאֲשֶׁר תָּאֹר יוּאָר.

6 וּבַיּוֹם הָרְבִיעִי נִקְהֲלוּ לְעֵמֶק בְּרָכָה.

7 בָּרוּךְ אַתָּה, יְיָ, הַמְבָרֵךְ אֶת עַמּוֹ יִשְׂרָאֵל בַּשָּׁלוֹם.

8 דָּבָר טוֹב וְקַיָּם לְעוֹלָם וָעֶד.

9 בָּרְכֵנוּ אָבִינוּ, כֻּלָּנוּ כְּאֶחָד, בְּאוֹר פָּנֶיךָ.

10 תְּהִלּוֹת לְאֵל עֶלְיוֹן, בָּרוּךְ הוּא וּמְבֹרָךְ.

11 יְיָ, צוּרִי וְגֹאֲלִי.

12 בָּרֵךְ עָלֵינוּ, יְיָ אֱלֹהֵינוּ, אֶת הַשָּׁנָה הַזֹּאת.

13

2   שְׁמַע

In ancient days, people believed in many different gods — a rain god, a sun god, a god of thunder, a god of fire.

Our ancestors were different because they believed that one God creates and rules everything and everyone.

The central prayer which states our belief in one unique God is the שְׁמַע.

The שְׁמַע is so important that it is often the first prayer that children learn.

The שְׁמַע is like a pledge of allegiance to God.

• • • • • • • • •

Practice reading the שְׁמַע aloud.

שְׁמַע יִשְׂרָאֵל: יְיָ אֱלֹהֵינוּ, יְיָ אֶחָד.

Hear O Israel: Adonai is our God, Adonai is One.

שְׁמַע
hear

_____

יִשְׂרָאֵל
Israel

_____

יְיָ
Adonai

_____

אֱלֹהֵינוּ
our God

_____

אֶחָד
one

What's Missing?

Complete each prayer phrase with the missing English word.

שְׁמַע   _____ O Israel

אֶחָד   Adonai is _____

יִשְׂרָאֵל   Hear O _____

יְיָ   _____ is our God

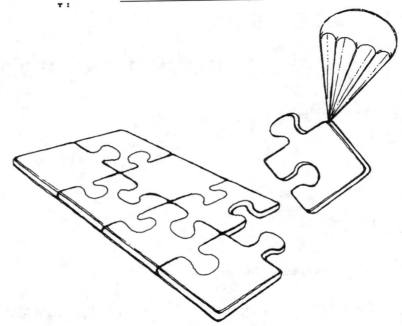

Unscramble the Prayer

Put the שְׁמַע in the correct order by numbering the words from 1 to 6.

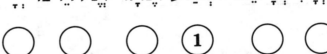

יְיָ יִשְׂרָאֵל שְׁמַע אֶחָד אֱלֹהֵינוּ יְיָ

◯   ◯   ◯   ①   ◯   ◯

15

In the Synagogue

The שְׁמַע is one of the most important prayers in Judaism. The words of the שְׁמַע are taken from the Book of Deuteronomy (דְּבָרִים) in the Torah. These words became part of our prayer service nearly 2,000 years ago.

The שְׁמַע appears in many places in the סִדוּר.
We say the words of the שְׁמַע in a loud and clear voice because it is so important.

When we declare

שְׁמַע יִשְׂרָאֵל: יְיָ אֱלֹהֵינוּ, יְיָ אֶחָד.

we are saying, *"We believe in one God."*

• • • • • • • • •

True or False

Put a ✔ next to each sentence that is true.

___ The שְׁמַע commands us to "hear" an important statement about God.

___ The שְׁמַע comes from the Book of Genesis in the Torah.

___ In the שְׁמַע we declare that we believe in one God.

___ There are many prayers that are more important than the שְׁמַע.

How do you think the שְׁמַע got its name?

_____

Word Hunt

Look across (◀) and down (▼) to find the Hebrew words.
Circle each word as you find it.

שְׁמַע · יִשְׂרָאֵל · יְיָ · אֱלֹהֵינוּ · יְיָ · אֶחָד

אֶ	ג	פ	טֶ	יִ	ב	ב	א
לֹ	צ	ק	מְ	יְ	ו	ר	לְ
הֵ	ו	י	אֶ	ג	ו	ךָ	עֲ
י	ל	אֵ	רָ	שִׁ	יִ	פ	הֶ
נ	ו	תֵ	עֲ	ב	ץ	מְ	ד
ו	ס	גֶ	יְ	יִ	ק	ז	שְׁ
ס	ח	א	בַ	ו	שׁ	נֵ	מַ
ט	ד	חָ	אֶ	וּ	נֶ	ף	ע

17

An Ethical Echo

The שְׁמַע prayer speaks directly to us. We are יִשְׂרָאֵל. We are the people of Israel. יִשְׂרָאֵל is also the name of the State of Israel. So the word יִשְׂרָאֵל means both the State of Israel and, in the שְׁמַע prayer, the people of Israel.

The Jewish people have an expression that all of יִשְׂרָאֵל is responsible for one another:

כָּל יִשְׂרָאֵל עֲרֵבִים זֶה בָּזֶה.

> **A Point to Ponder**
> Why is it especially important for the Jewish people to be responsible for one another?

• • • • • • • • • •

Family Letters

The words below contain the family letters שׁ and שׂ.
Practice reading the words below.

שֵׁשֶׁת	שֵׁשׁ	שֵׁם	שְׁמוֹ	שְׁמַע	שָׁלוֹם	1
שֶׁעָשָׂה	יִשְׂרָאֵל	עָשָׂה	שָׁם	שְׂאוּ	שָׂשׂוֹן	2
מֹשֶׁה	לַעֲשׂוֹת	רֹאשׁ	שָׁלֹשׁ	שִׂים	שָׂמֵחַ	3

• • • • • • • • • •

Did You Know?

If you look inside a mezuzah (מְזוּזָה), you will find the שְׁמַע prayer written on the piece of parchment inside.

Why is the שְׁמַע inside the mezuzah? Because the paragraph that follows the שְׁמַע — the וְאָהַבְתָּ — tells us to "write these words on the doorposts of your home."

18

Word Endings

The word אֱלֹהֵינוּ is made up of two parts:

אֱלֹהֵי   means "God of."

נוּ   is an ending that means "us" or "our."

אֱלֹהֵינוּ   means "our God."

• • • • • • • • •

Circle the Hebrew word that means "our God" in the following prayer:

שְׁמַע יִשְׂרָאֵל: יְיָ אֱלֹהֵינוּ, יְיָ אֶחָד.

Write the ending that means "us" or "our." _____

Write the Hebrew word that means "our God." _____

Because our ancestors were the first to know that God was the One God of all the world, we feel especially close to God and so we say "*our* God."

Reading Practice

Practice reading the following סִדוּר phrases.
Circle the word אֱלֹהֵינוּ wherever it appears.

1   רְצֵה יְיָ אֱלֹהֵינוּ בְּעַמְּךָ יִשְׂרָאֵל.

2   בָּרֵךְ עָלֵינוּ, יְיָ אֱלֹהֵינוּ, אֶת הַשָּׁנָה הַזֹּאת.

3   אַהֲבָה רַבָּה אֲהַבְתָּנוּ, יְיָ אֱלֹהֵינוּ.

4   הַשְׁכִּיבֵנוּ יְיָ אֱלֹהֵינוּ לְשָׁלוֹם.

In each of the sentences above, the Hebrew word for Adonai also appears.

Write the Hebrew word for Adonai _____

• • • • • • • • •

Fluent Reading

Each phrase contains a word you know. Practice reading the lines below.

● ● ● ● ● ● ● ● ●

1 שְׁמַע יִשְׂרָאֵל: יְיָ אֱלֹהֵינוּ, יְיָ אֶחָד.

2 אֶחָד הוּא אֱלֹהֵינוּ, הוּא אָבִינוּ, הוּא מַלְכֵּנוּ.

3 אֶחָד אֱלֹהֵינוּ, גָּדוֹל אֲדוֹנֵינוּ, קָדוֹשׁ שְׁמוֹ.

4 וְהוּא אֶחָד, וְאֵין שֵׁנִי.

5 בַּיּוֹם הַהוּא יִהְיֶה יְיָ אֶחָד וּשְׁמוֹ אֶחָד.

6 שָׁלוֹם רָב עַל יִשְׂרָאֵל עַמֶּךָ.

7 צוּר יִשְׂרָאֵל, קוּמָה בְּעֶזְרַת יִשְׂרָאֵל.

8 שְׁמַע! בַּיָּמִים הָהֵם בַּזְּמַן הַזֶּה.

9 שְׁמַע, וְהָיָה אִם שָׁמֹעַ.

10 אַהֲבָה רַבָּה אֲהַבְתָּנוּ, יְיָ אֱלֹהֵינוּ.

11 וַיְהִי עֶרֶב וַיְהִי בֹקֶר, יוֹם אֶחָד.

21

3

Throughout history, in every country where the Jewish people have lived, they have seen rulers rise — and fade from power.

Only one Ruler has remained constant.

The second line of the שְׁמַע states our belief that יְיָ is the only true and eternal Ruler of יִשְׂרָאֵל.

• • • • • • • • •

The first line of the שְׁמַע is said in a loud and clear voice.

שְׁמַע יִשְׂרָאֵל: יְיָ אֱלֹהֵינוּ, יְיָ אֶחָד.

Hear O Israel: Adonai is our God, Adonai is One.

These words come from the Book of Deuteronomy in the Bible.

The second line of the שְׁמַע is spoken quietly.

בָּרוּךְ שֵׁם כְּבוֹד מַלְכוּתוֹ לְעוֹלָם וָעֶד.

Blessed is the name of God's glorious kingdom forever and ever.

These words are not from the Bible. They were first recited in the ancient Temple in Jerusalem. They later became the *response* to the first line of the שְׁמַע prayer.

Practice reading the שְׁמַע aloud.

1 שְׁמַע יִשְׂרָאֵל: יְיָ אֱלֹהֵינוּ, יְיָ אֶחָד.

2 בָּרוּךְ שֵׁם כְּבוֹד מַלְכוּתוֹ לְעוֹלָם וָעֶד.

Word Match

Match the English word(s) to its Hebrew meaning.

A. forever and ever

B. blessed

C. God's kingdom

D. name

E. glory of

( ) בָּרוּךְ

( ) שֵׁם

( ) כְּבוֹד

( ) מַלְכוּתוֹ

( ) לְעוֹלָם וָעֶד

בָּרוּךְ
blessed, praised

שֵׁם
name

כְּבוֹד
glory of

מַלְכוּתוֹ
God's kingdom

לְעוֹלָם וָעֶד
forever and
ever

What's Missing?

Complete each prayer phrase with the missing Hebrew word(s).

בָּרוּךְ _____ כְּבוֹד   name

_____ _____ מַלְכוּתוֹ.   forever and ever

שֵׁם כְּבוֹד _____   blessed

כְּבוֹד _____ לְעוֹלָם וָעֶד.   God's kingdom

True or False

Put a ✔ next to each sentence that is true.

____ The first line of the שְׁמַע is said in a loud voice.

____ The second part of the שְׁמַע comes from the Bible.

____ We say the second part of the שְׁמַע in a soft voice.

____ The ancient Temple stood in Jerusalem.

____ יְיָ is the only true Ruler of יִשְׂרָאֵל.

Look Alikes

These two letters — צ and ע — look similar, but are pronounced differently.

Each word below contains one of these letters.
Practice reading the words below.

1 בְּעֶזְרַת עָלֵינוּ עַמְּךָ שְׁמַע לְעוֹלָם מֵעַתָּה

2 צוּר לִיצִיאַת בְּרָצוֹן צְבָאוֹת וְצֶדֶק הָאָרֶץ

3 לְמַעַן רָצִיתָ בְּמִצְרַיִם עַל בַּעֲבוּר מִצְוֹת

4 שַׁוְעָתָם בְּצֵאתָם בְּרַעַשׁ עוֹלָם וּמַצָּה הַמּוֹצִיא

Word Endings

The word מַלְכוּתוֹ appears in the second line of the שְׁמַע.
The word מַלְכוּתוֹ is made up of two parts:

מַלְכוּת means "kingdom."

וֹ is an ending that means "his."

מַלְכוּתוֹ means "His kingdom" or "God's kingdom."

As God is neither male nor female, we translate the word מַלְכוּתוֹ as *God's kingdom.*

• • • • • • • • •

Circle the word that means *God's kingdom* in the following prayer:

בָּרוּךְ שֵׁם כְּבוֹד מַלְכוּתוֹ לְעוֹלָם וָעֶד.

Write the Hebrew word that means *God's kingdom.* _____

25

Roots

מַלְכוּתוֹ is built on the root מלכ (or מלך).

The root מלכ means king or ruler. The three letters מלכ tell us that king or ruler is part of a word's meaning.

• • • • • • • • •

Circle the three root letters in this word.

מַלְכוּתוֹ

Write the root _____ _____ _____

What does the root mean? _____

Circle the three root letters in each of these words.

תִּמְלֹךְ   מַלְכָּה   מַלְכוּת   מַלְכֵּנוּ   מֶלֶךְ

• • • • • • • • •

Did You Know?

We say, בָּרוּךְ שֵׁם כְּבוֹד מַלְכוּתוֹ לְעוֹלָם וָעֶד in a quiet voice.

Why?

During the time when the Roman Empire ruled the Land of Israel, it was forbidden to praise any kings other than the Roman emperors. Rome sent spies to the synagogues to listen to the prayers, so the Jews would whisper the words that praised God as Ruler forever and ever.

Can you think of another example of people who might have to whisper to protect themselves?

26

וְאָהַבְתָּ

The שְׁמַע is followed by a prayer called וְאָהַבְתָּ.

The שְׁמַע and the וְאָהַבְתָּ both come from the book of Deuteronomy (דְּבָרִים) in the Torah.

In the וְאָהַבְתָּ we are told to love God with all of our being. We show our love for God by following God's laws and commandments and by teaching them to our children.

Practice reading the וְאָהַבְתָּ.

1 וְאָהַבְתָּ אֵת יְיָ אֱלֹהֶיךָ

2 בְּכָל־לְבָבְךָ וּבְכָל־נַפְשְׁךָ וּבְכָל־מְאֹדֶךָ.

3 וְהָיוּ הַדְּבָרִים הָאֵלֶּה, אֲשֶׁר אָנֹכִי מְצַוְּךָ הַיּוֹם, עַל־לְבָבֶךָ.

4 וְשִׁנַּנְתָּם לְבָנֶיךָ, וְדִבַּרְתָּ בָּם בְּשִׁבְתְּךָ בְּבֵיתֶךָ,

5 וּבְלֶכְתְּךָ בַדֶּרֶךְ, וּבְשָׁכְבְּךָ וּבְקוּמֶךָ.

6 וּקְשַׁרְתָּם לְאוֹת עַל־יָדֶךָ, וְהָיוּ לְטֹטָפֹת בֵּין עֵינֶיךָ.

7 וּכְתַבְתָּם עַל־מְזֻזוֹת בֵּיתֶךָ וּבִשְׁעָרֶיךָ.

And you shall love Adonai, your God,
with all your heart, and with all your soul, and with all your might.
Set these words, which I command you this day, upon your heart.
Teach them to your children, and speak of them when you are at home,
and when you go on your way, and when you lie down, and when you get up.
Bind them as a sign upon your hand and let them be symbols between your eyes.
Inscribe them on the doorposts of your house and on your gates.

Some congregations add these words at the end of the וְאָהַבְתָּ.

1 לְמַעַן תִּזְכְּרוּ וַעֲשִׂיתֶם אֶת־כָּל־מִצְוֹתָי, וִהְיִיתֶם קְדֹשִׁים

2 לֵאלֹהֵיכֶם. אֲנִי יְיָ אֱלֹהֵיכֶם, אֲשֶׁר הוֹצֵאתִי אֶתְכֶם מֵאֶרֶץ

3 מִצְרַיִם לִהְיוֹת לָכֶם לֵאלֹהִים. אֲנִי יְיָ אֱלֹהֵיכֶם.

And You Shall Love Adonai...

The theme of וְאָהַבְתָּ is our love for God. Look at the names of these three prayers having to do with the love between God and the Jewish people.

אַהֲבָה רַבָּה   אַהֲבַת עוֹלָם   וְאָהַבְתָּ

Do you notice a common root?
The root אהב means *love*.

Read the following prayer excerpts and circle all the words with the root אהב.

1. הַבּוֹחֵר בְּעַמּוֹ יִשְׂרָאֵל בְּאַהֲבָה

2. אַהֲבַת עוֹלָם בֵּית יִשְׂרָאֵל עַמְּךָ אָהָבְתָּ

3. וְיַחֵד לְבָבֵנוּ לְאַהֲבָה וּלְיִרְאָה אֶת שְׁמֶךָ

4. בְּאַהֲבָה וּבְרָצוֹן שַׁבַּת קָדְשֶׁךָ

5. אַהֲבָה רַבָּה אֲהַבְתָּנוּ יְיָ אֱלֹהֵינוּ

6. כָּל דִּבְרֵי תַלְמוּד תּוֹרָתֶךָ בְּאַהֲבָה

וְאָהַבְתָּ tells us to reciprocate God's love for us. Write one way that we can show our love of God.

_____

_____

An Ethical Echo

In the Jewish tradition there is a saying that *Talmud Torah* — the Study of the Torah — is more important than anything:

תַּלְמוּד תּוֹרָה כְּנֶגֶד כֻּלָּם.

Since both the שְׁמַע and the וְאָהַבְתָּ prayers are taken from the Torah, when you say these prayers you are studying the Torah. So reciting the שְׁמַע actually helps you fulfill the mitzvah it asks you to do!

A Point to Ponder

It is not enough just to *study* Torah; it is just as important to *do* Torah (perform God's mitzvot).

Why are studying the Torah and fulfilling its commandments *both* essential elements of *Talmud Torah*? How do they help you to be a better person?

Fluent Reading

Each phrase contains a word you know. Practice reading the lines below.

• • • • • • • • •

1   בָּרוּךְ שֵׁם כְּבוֹד מַלְכוּתוֹ לְעוֹלָם וָעֶד.

2   הַלְלוּ, עַבְדֵי יְיָ, הַלְלוּ אֶת שֵׁם יְיָ.

3   וְלֹא נֵבוֹשׁ לְעוֹלָם וָעֶד, כִּי בְשֵׁם קָדְשְׁךָ....

4   וְטוֹב וְיָפֶה הַדָּבָר הַזֶּה עָלֵינוּ לְעוֹלָם וָעֶד.

5   שָׁאַתָּה הוּא יְיָ אֱלֹהֵינוּ וֵאלֹהֵי אֲבוֹתֵינוּ לְעוֹלָם וָעֶד.

6   קָדוֹשׁ, קָדוֹשׁ, קָדוֹשׁ יְיָ צְבָאוֹת, מְלֹא כָל הָאָרֶץ כְּבוֹדוֹ.

7   לֹא תִשָּׂא אֶת שֵׁם יְהוָה אֱלֹהֶיךָ לַשָּׁוְא.

8   הָבוּ לַיְיָ כְּבוֹד שְׁמוֹ.

9   מִמִּזְרַח שֶׁמֶשׁ עַד מְבוֹאוֹ מְהֻלָּל שֵׁם יְיָ.

מִי כָמֹכָה

4

More than three thousand years ago the Jewish people were slaves in the land of Egypt. It was a time of great suffering and pain. But God freed our people from slavery.

When the Children of Israel left Egypt, the Egyptian army chased after them. They followed our people to the edge of a large sea — the Sea of Reeds. There was no way to escape. But God sent a great wind. It pushed apart the waters of the sea and our people crossed safely on dry land. They were so happy to be free that they celebrated with a song of thanks to God.

Below are three lines from that song. It is called מִי כָמֹכָה. When you read the prayer, you will be reciting the very same words the Jewish people sang over three thousand years ago. Imagine the joy of the people who were free for the first time. Imagine how grateful they were to God.

● ● ● ● ● ● ● ● ●

Practice reading מִי כָמֹכָה aloud.

Who is like You among the gods, Adonai?	מִי־כָמֹכָה בָּאֵלִם, יְיָ? 1
Who is like You, majestic in holiness,	מִי כָּמֹכָה, נֶאְדָּר בַּקֹּדֶשׁ, 2
Awesome in splendor, doing wonders?	נוֹרָא תְהִלֹת, עֹשֵׂה פֶלֶא? 3

Search and Circle

Circle the Hebrew word(s) that means the same as the English.

English			
like You	סִדּוּר	כָּמֹכָה	שְׁמַע
Adonai	מִי	בָּאֵלִם	יְיָ
majestic	בַּקֹּדֶשׁ	יִשְׂרָאֵל	נֶאְדָּר
who	מִי	אֶחָד	שֵׁם
in holiness	בָּרְכוּ	בַּקֹּדֶשׁ	בָּאֵלִם
among the gods	בָּאֵלִם	הַמְבֹרָךְ	לְעוֹלָם וָעֶד

Prayer Dictionary (side column)

מִי
who

כָּמֹכָה, כָּמֹכָה
like you

בָּאֵלִם
among the gods

יְיָ
Adonai

נֶאְדָּר
majestic

בַּקֹּדֶשׁ
in holiness

31

Understanding the Prayer

מִי־כָמֹכָה בָּאֵלִם, יְיָ?

מִי כָּמֹכָה, נֶאְדָּר בַּקֹּדֶשׁ

• • • • • • • • •

1. Underline the words that mean "Who is like you."

2. Draw a ✡ over the Hebrew word for "in holiness."

3. Circle the word that means "among the gods."

4. Draw a squiggly line under the word that means "majestic."

5. Draw a triangle around the Hebrew word for "Adonai."

6. Write the two words that appear in both lines.

_____

7. What is the English meaning of these words?

_____

Did You Know?

The rabbis tell us that the word אֵלִם (gods) is deliberately misspelled in the מִי כָמֹכָה. The י before the ם is left out. This shows us that the other "gods" were faulty or imperfect. יְיָ is the one, true God.

The Holiday Connection

The Maccabees were a brave group of Jews who fought the Syrian king Antiochus and his army. Antiochus would not let the Jewish people study Torah. They were not permitted to worship God or celebrate the Jewish holidays.

You already know that we celebrate the victory of the Maccabees on Ḥanukkah. But do you know how the Maccabees got their name?

Legend has it that when Judah Maccabee, the leader of the Jewish soldiers, called the Jews to battle, he cried מִי כָמֹכָה בָּאֵלִם יְיָ.
The Jews rallied to his side.

● ● ● ● ● ● ● ● ●

Write the first letter of each Hebrew word in the spaces below.

מִי כָמֹכָה בָּאֵלִם יְיָ

___ ___ ___ ___

What does this word spell?

Why do you think Judah chose this prayer to rally the Jews together?

An Ethical Echo
Throughout the ages the Jewish people have experienced captivity and freedom, slavery and independence. We know how precious freedom is. And we are determined to help those who are not free.

We call this the mitzvah of *Pidyon Shevuyim* פִּדְיוֹן שְׁבוּיִים — Redeeming the Captive.

A Point to Ponder
Think about the ways that we try to bring freedom to other people in the world.

In the Synagogue

The prayer מִי כָמֹכָה is from the Torah. It appears in the Book of Exodus. Exodus tells the story of our people's journey from slavery in Egypt to freedom. מִי כָמֹכָה appears after the Children of Israel have safely crossed the Sea of Reeds.

Today, מִי כָמֹכָה is read at both the morning and evening services in the synagogue. The first three lines and the last line of the prayer are identical in both services.

• • • • • • • • •

Practice reading the first three lines of מִי כָמֹכָה.

1 מִי־כָמֹכָה בָּאֵלִם, יְיָ? *Who is like You among the gods, Adonai?*

2 מִי כָּמֹכָה, נֶאְדָּר בַּקֹּדֶשׁ, *Who is like You, majestic in holiness,*

3 נוֹרָא תְהִלֹּת, עֹשֵׂה פֶלֶא? *Awesome in splendor, doing wonders?*

Now read the last line of מִי כָמֹכָה.

יְיָ יִמְלֹךְ לְעוֹלָם וָעֶד.

Adonai will rule forever and ever.

Which three letters in יִמְלֹךְ tell us that ruler is part of the word's meaning? Write the three letters.

_____ _____ _____

These three letters are called the _____.

Write the phrase that means "forever and ever." _____

34

True or False

Put a ✔ next to each sentence that is true.

___ In the מִי כָמֹכָה we say that there is none greater than God.

___ מִי כָמֹכָה is only read once a day in the synagogue.

___ מִי כָמֹכָה was first sung when the Children of Israel crossed the Sea of Reeds.

___ מִי כָמֹכָה comes from the Book of Genesis in the Torah.

___ מִי כָמֹכָה is a song of thanks to God.

Roots

The word בַּקֹדֶשׁ is built on the root קדשׁ.
The root קדשׁ means "holy."
The root קדשׁ tells us that "holy" is part of a word's meaning.

● ● ● ● ● ● ● ● ●

Circle the three root letters in this word.

בַּקֹדֶשׁ

Write the root _____ _____ _____

What does the root mean? _____

Circle the three root letters in each of these words.

קִדְשָׁנוּ   קָדֹשׁוֹ   וְתִתְקַדַּשׁ   הַקָּדוֹשׁ   קָדְשׁוֹ   קָדוֹשׁ

What's Inside?

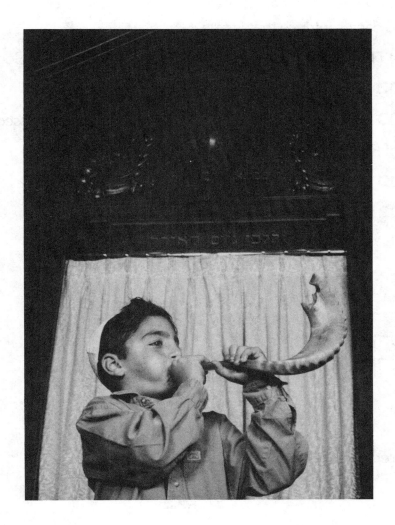

This boy is blowing a shofar in front of the Holy Ark.

Do you know what is kept inside the Holy Ark?

_____

Complete the Hebrew name for the Holy Ark by writing the root for "holy" in the blanks below.

אֲרוֹן הַ_____ _____ _____

Back to the Sources

This is a page from the Book of Exodus in the Torah. It is the song the Jews sang after they crossed the Sea of Reeds.

1. Can you find and read the first three lines of מִי כָמֹכָה?
2. Can you find and read the last line of מִי כָמֹכָה?

אָמַר

אוֹיֵב אֶרְדֹּף אַשִּׂיג   אֲחַלֵּק שָׁלָל תִּמְלָאֵמוֹ

י נַפְשִׁי   אָרִיק חַרְבִּי תּוֹרִישֵׁמוֹ יָדִי: נָשַׁפְתָּ

בְרוּחֲךָ כִּסָּמוֹ יָם   צָלֲלוּ כַּעוֹפֶרֶת בְּמַיִם

11 אַדִּירִים: מִי־כָמֹכָה בָּאֵלִם יְהֹוָה   מִי

כָּמֹכָה נֶאְדָּר בַּקֹּדֶשׁ   נוֹרָא תְהִלֹּת עֹשֵׂה־

12 13 פֶלֶא: נָטִיתָ יְמִינְךָ תִּבְלָעֵמוֹ אָרֶץ: נָחִיתָ

בְחַסְדְּךָ עַם־זוּ גָּאָלְתָּ   נֵהַלְתָּ בְעָזְּךָ אֶל־נְוֵה

14 קָדְשֶׁךָ:   שָׁמְעוּ עַמִּים יִרְגָּזוּן   חִיל

טו אָחַז יֹשְׁבֵי פְּלָשֶׁת: אָז נִבְהֲלוּ אַלּוּפֵי

אֱדוֹם   אֵילֵי מוֹאָב יֹאחֲזֵמוֹ רָעַד   נָמֹגוּ

16 כֹּל יֹשְׁבֵי כְנָעַן: תִּפֹּל עֲלֵיהֶם אֵימָתָה

וָפַחַד   בִּגְדֹל זְרוֹעֲךָ יִדְּמוּ כָּאָבֶן   עַד־

יַעֲבֹר עַמְּךָ יְהֹוָה   עַד־יַעֲבֹר עַם־זוּ

17 קָנִיתָ:   תְּבִאֵמוֹ וְתִטָּעֵמוֹ בְּהַר נַחֲלָתְךָ   מָכוֹן

לְשִׁבְתְּךָ פָּעַלְתָּ יְהֹוָה   מִקְּדָשׁ אֲדֹנָי כּוֹנְנוּ

18 19 יָדֶיךָ:   יְהֹוָה ׀ יִמְלֹךְ לְעֹלָם וָעֶד:

Prayer Building Blocks

בְּקֹדֶשׁ "in holiness"

....

בְּקֹדֶשׁ   means "in holiness."

בְּקֹדֶשׁ   is made up of two parts:

בְּ   means "in the."

קֹדֶשׁ   means "holiness."

Circle the word part that means "in the."   בְּקֹדֶשׁ

Write the word part that means "in the." _____

בָּאֵלִם "among the gods"

....

בָּאֵלִם   means "among the gods."

בָּאֵלִם   is made up of two parts:

בָּ   means "among the" or "in (the)."

אֵלִם   means "gods," the many false gods that people worshipped.

Circle the part of the word that means "among the" or "in the."   בָּאֵלִם

Write the word part that means "among the" or "in the." _____

Reading Practice

Practice reading these words.
Circle the word parts that mean "in" or "in the."

1	בְּקֹדֶשׁ	בָּאֵלִם	בְּחֶסֶד	בְּקֹדְשָׁתוֹ	בְּכָל
2	בָּאלֹהִים	בְּחֵן	בִּמְרוֹמָיו	בַּיָּמִים	בַּזְּמַן

38

Fluent Reading

Each phrase contains a word you know. Practice reading the lines below.

• • • • • • • • •

1 מִי־כָמְכָה בָּאֵלִם, יְיָ?

2 מִי כָּמְכָה, נֶאְדָּר בַּקֹּדֶשׁ,

3 נוֹרָא תְהִלֹּת, עֹשֵׂה פֶלֶא?

4 מִי כָמְוֹךָ, בַּעַל גְּבוּרוֹת, וּמִי דוֹמֶה לָּךְ.

5 אֵין כָּמוֹךָ חַנּוּן וְרַחוּם, יְיָ אֱלֹהֵינוּ.

6 אֵין כָּמוֹךָ, אֵל, אֶרֶךְ אַפַּיִם וְרַב חֶסֶד וֶאֱמֶת.

7 רַחֵם עָלֵינוּ וְעַל כָּל מַעֲשֶׂיךָ, כִּי אֵין כָּמוֹךָ, יְיָ אֱלֹהֵינוּ.

8 תְּהִלַּת יְיָ יְדַבֶּר פִּי, וִיבָרֵךְ כָּל בָּשָׂר שֵׁם קָדְשׁוֹ.

9 מִי יַעֲלֶה בְהַר יְיָ, וּמִי יָקוּם בִּמְקוֹם קָדְשׁוֹ?

10 וְאַתָּה קָדוֹשׁ, יוֹשֵׁב תְּהִלּוֹת יִשְׂרָאֵל.

When a friend gives you a gift, you say thank you. You want to show your appreciation, and acknowledge your friend's generosity.

We have a special way of saying thank you for God's gifts. We say a בְּרָכָה — words of praise and thanks to God.

There are many different kinds of בְּרָכוֹת: blessings over wine, Shabbat candles, cake and fruit. There is a בְּרָכָה for when we get something new, a בְּרָכָה for when we get up in the morning, and one to say when we see a rainbow. There is even a בְּרָכָה to say when we see lightning or an unusual natural sight, like the Grand Canyon.

In addition to thanking יְיָ, a בְּרָכָה reminds us that יְיָ created the special thing we are about to enjoy.

Most בְּרָכוֹת begin with the same six Hebrew words.

• • • • • • • • •

Practice reading these six words.

בָּרוּךְ אַתָּה, יְיָ אֱלֹהֵינוּ, מֶלֶךְ הָעוֹלָם

Praised are You, Adonai our God, Ruler of the world

PRAYER DICTIONARY

בָּרוּךְ
praised, blessed

אַתָּה
you

יְיָ
Adonai

אֱלֹהֵינוּ
our God

מֶלֶךְ
ruler

הָעוֹלָם
the world

Search and Circle

Circle the Hebrew word that means the same as the English.

English			
Adonai	שֵׁם	יְיָ	אַתָּה
ruler	מֶלֶךְ	כָּבוֹד	יִשְׂרָאֵל
the world	נֶאְדָּר	הָעוֹלָם	כָּמְכָה
our God	בָּאֵלִם	מַלְכוּתוֹ	אֱלֹהֵינוּ
praised	שְׁמַע	בַּקֹּדֶשׁ	בָּרוּךְ
you	אַתָּה	מִי	אֶחָד

41

Beginnings and Endings

For each blessing underline the six words that usually begin a בְּרָכָה.

1 בָּרוּךְ אַתָּה, יְיָ אֱלֹהֵינוּ, מֶלֶךְ הָעוֹלָם, בּוֹרֵא פְּרִי הַגָּפֶן.

2 בָּרוּךְ אַתָּה, יְיָ אֱלֹהֵינוּ, מֶלֶךְ הָעוֹלָם, הַמּוֹצִיא לֶחֶם מִן הָאָרֶץ.

3 בָּרוּךְ אַתָּה, יְיָ אֱלֹהֵינוּ, מֶלֶךְ הָעוֹלָם, בּוֹרֵא מִינֵי מְזוֹנוֹת.

Now *write* the words that usually begin a בְּרָכָה.

_____

The first six words of a blessing are usually the same, but the ending changes according to what you are thanking God for.

Circle the endings of the three blessings above.

Which of these blessings is said over ḥallah? Write the number: _____

More בְּרָכוֹת Practice

Below are a few of the בְּרָכוֹת that are most regularly recited.
Practice reading the blessings.

1   בָּרוּךְ אַתָּה, יְיָ אֱלֹהֵינוּ, מֶלֶךְ הָעוֹלָם, בּוֹרֵא פְּרִי הָעֵץ.

Praised are You, Adonai our God, Ruler of the world, who creates the fruit of the tree.

2   בָּרוּךְ אַתָּה, יְיָ אֱלֹהֵינוּ, מֶלֶךְ הָעוֹלָם, בּוֹרֵא מְאוֹרֵי הָאֵשׁ.

Praised are You, Adonai our God, Ruler of the world, who creates the light of the fire.

3   בָּרוּךְ אַתָּה, יְיָ אֱלֹהֵינוּ, מֶלֶךְ הָעוֹלָם, בּוֹרֵא פְּרִי הָאֲדָמָה.

Praised are You, Adonai our God, Ruler of the world, who creates the fruit of the earth.

4   בָּרוּךְ אַתָּה, יְיָ אֱלֹהֵינוּ, מֶלֶךְ הָעוֹלָם, שֶׁהֶחֱיָנוּ וְקִיְּמָנוּ וְהִגִּיעָנוּ לַזְּמַן הַזֶּה.

Praised are You, Adonai our God, Ruler of the world, who has given us life and sustained us, and permitted us to reach this season.

Do you know which of these blessings is said before eating a peach?
(Hint: What does a peach grow on?)

Write the number of the blessing here: _____

Six in a Row

Draw a line to connect the six words that begin בְּרָכוֹת. Start with the word בָּרוּךְ and finish at הָעוֹלָם. Do not cross any solid lines.

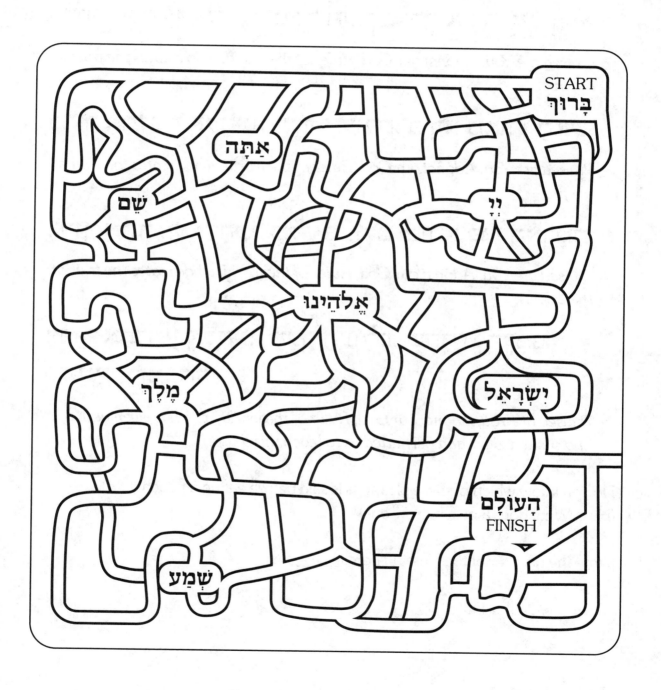

Prayer Building Blocks

בָּרוּךְ "blessed" or "praised"

בָּרוּךְ may come from the Hebrew word בֶּרֶךְ, "knee."

בָּרוּךְ reminds us that praising or blessing Adonai is like kneeling in front of a ruler. When we say a בְּרָכָה it is as if we are kneeling in front of Adonai, our Ruler.

בָּרוּךְ is built on the root _____ _____ _____ .

בֶּרֶךְ is built on the root _____ _____ _____ .

בְּרָכָה is built on the root _____ _____ _____ .

This root means "blessed" or "praised."

אַתָּה "you"

When we say a blessing we speak directly to God. We use the Hebrew word אַתָּה to address God. We talk to God as a friend who is near us.

The Hebrew word for "you" is _____ .
Fill in the missing word below.

בָּרוּךְ _____ יְיָ אֱלֹהֵינוּ מֶלֶךְ הָעוֹלָם

45

מֶלֶךְ "ruler"

In a בְּרָכָה we call God "You," just as we would a friend. But a moment later we address God as "Ruler." We have many kinds of relationships with God.

God is our friend and our ruler.

The word מֶלֶךְ literally means king. Because God is neither male nor female, we translate מֶלֶךְ as "ruler."

מֶלֶךְ is built on the root _____ _____ _____ .

This root means _____ .

In each of the words below circle the three root letters. (Hint: כ ך are family letters.)

מַלְכוּתְךָ   מֶלֶךְ   הַמְּלָכִים   מַלְכֵי

הָעוֹלָם "the world" "the universe"

God is not just Ruler of the Jewish people, God is Ruler of the whole world.

הָעוֹלָם   means "the world" or "the universe."

עוֹלָם   means "world" or "universe."

הָ   means "the."

Circle the part of each Hebrew word which means "the" in each example below.

הָעוֹלָם   הָאָרֶץ   הַגֶּפֶן   הָעֵץ   הָאֲדָמָה

What does הָ mean? _____ .

Did You Know?

The Rabbis of long ago told us that we should say one hundred blessings a day. One hundred blessings in *one* day?

In fact, if you added up all the בְּרָכוֹת in the three daily synagogue services plus some of the extra blessings said during the day, you would easily reach one hundred.

• • • • • • • • •

An Ethical Echo

Saying a בְּרָכָה makes us stop and appreciate the world around us. We thank God, and show that we do not take God's creations for granted. We are the caretakers of God's world. We show our respect for God by treating God's world — our earth — with respect. In the Torah, this commandment is called *Bal Tashḥit* — בַּל תַּשְׁחִית — Preserving the Earth.

A Point to Ponder
Can you think of ways to treat the earth with respect?

47

Blessing Match

Draw a line between the blessing and its matching picture.

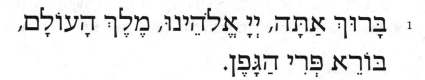

1

בָּרוּךְ אַתָּה, יְיָ אֱלֹהֵינוּ, מֶלֶךְ הָעוֹלָם,
בּוֹרֵא פְּרִי הַגָּפֶן.

*Praised are You, Adonai our God, Ruler of the world,
who creates the fruit of the vine.*

2

בָּרוּךְ אַתָּה, יְיָ אֱלֹהֵינוּ, מֶלֶךְ הָעוֹלָם,
הַמּוֹצִיא לֶחֶם מִן הָאָרֶץ.

*Praised are You, Adonai our God, Ruler of the world,
who brings forth bread from the earth.*

3

בָּרוּךְ אַתָּה, יְיָ אֱלֹהֵינוּ, מֶלֶךְ הָעוֹלָם,
בּוֹרֵא פְּרִי הָאֲדָמָה.

*Praised are You, Adonai our God, Ruler of the world,
who creates the fruit of the earth.*

4

בָּרוּךְ אַתָּה, יְיָ אֱלֹהֵינוּ, מֶלֶךְ הָעוֹלָם,
בּוֹרֵא מִינֵי מְזוֹנוֹת.

*Praised are You, Adonai our God, Ruler of the world,
who creates various foods.*

Fluent Reading

Each sentence contains a word you know. Practice reading the lines below.

● ● ● ● ● ● ● ● ●

1 בָּרוּךְ שֶׁאָמַר וְהָיָה הָעוֹלָם, בָּרוּךְ הוּא.

2 בָּרוּךְ אַתָּה, יְיָ אֱלֹהֵינוּ, מֶלֶךְ הָעוֹלָם,
הַזָּן אֶת הָעוֹלָם כֻּלּוֹ בְּטוּבוֹ, בְּחֵן בְּחֶסֶד וּבְרַחֲמִים.

3 בָּרוּךְ אַתָּה, יְיָ אֱלֹהֵינוּ, מֶלֶךְ הָעוֹלָם,
שֶׁעָשָׂה נִסִּים לַאֲבוֹתֵינוּ בַּיָּמִים הָהֵם בַּזְּמַן הַזֶּה.

4 בָּרוּךְ כְּבוֹד יְיָ מִמְּקוֹמוֹ.

5 בָּרוּךְ אַתָּה, יְיָ אֱלֹהֵינוּ, מֶלֶךְ הָעוֹלָם,
בּוֹרֵא מִינֵי בְשָׂמִים.

6 בָּרוּךְ אַתָּה, יְיָ, מְקַדֵּשׁ הַשַּׁבָּת וְיִשְׂרָאֵל וְהַזְּמַנִּים.

7 בָּרוּךְ אַתָּה, יְיָ אֱלֹהֵינוּ, מֶלֶךְ הָעוֹלָם, דַּיַּן הָאֱמֶת.

8 בָּרוּךְ אַתָּה, יְיָ, הַזָּן אֶת הַכֹּל.

49

We say certain blessings to remind us that we are fulfilling one of God's commandments, a מִצְוָה. These blessings are called *blessings of mitzvah*, בְּרכוֹת שֶׁל מִצְוָה.

Studying the Torah, sitting in the sukkah, and eating matzah at the Pesaḥ seder are all examples of these *mitzvot*.

• • • • • • • • •

Every בְּרָכָה שֶׁל מִצְוָה begins with the same ten words.
Practice reading these words.

1   בָּרוּךְ אַתָּה, יְיָ אֱלֹהֵינוּ, מֶלֶךְ הָעוֹלָם,

2   אֲשֶׁר קִדְּשָׁנוּ בְּמִצְוֹתָיו וְצִוָּנוּ

Praised are You, Adonai our God, Ruler of the world, who makes us holy with commandments and commands us...

אֲשֶׁר

who

קִדְּשָׁנוּ

makes us holy

בְּמִצְוֹתָיו

with God's
commandments

וְצִוָּנוּ

and commands us

Word Match

Match the English word to its Hebrew meaning.

A. with God's commandments

B. who

C. and commands us

D. makes us holy

E. the world

אֲשֶׁר ( )

קִדְּשָׁנוּ ( )

בְּמִצְוֹתָיו ( )

וְצִוָּנוּ ( )

הָעוֹלָם ( )

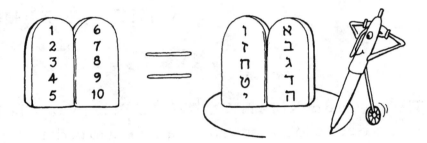

Did You Notice?

There are four words that help us to recognize a
בְּרָכָה שֶׁל מִצְוָה. The words are:

אֲשֶׁר קִדְּשָׁנוּ בְּמִצְוֹתָיו וְצִוָּנוּ

• • • • • • • • •

Fill in the words that always begin a בְּרָכָה שֶׁל מִצְוָה.

בָּרוּךְ אַתָּה, יְיָ אֱלֹהֵינוּ, מֶלֶךְ הָעוֹלָם

_____ _____ _____

Reading Practice

Read the following בְּרָכוֹת שֶׁל מִצְוָה aloud.
For each blessing underline the ten words that always begin a בְּרָכָה שֶׁל מִצְוָה.

1   בָּרוּךְ אַתָּה, יְיָ אֱלֹהֵינוּ, מֶלֶךְ הָעוֹלָם, אֲשֶׁר קִדְּשָׁנוּ
בְּמִצְוֹתָיו וְצִוָּנוּ לְהַדְלִיק נֵר שֶׁל שַׁבָּת.

2   בָּרוּךְ אַתָּה, יְיָ אֱלֹהֵינוּ, מֶלֶךְ הָעוֹלָם, אֲשֶׁר קִדְּשָׁנוּ
בְּמִצְוֹתָיו וְצִוָּנוּ עַל נְטִילַת יָדָיִם.

3   בָּרוּךְ אַתָּה, יְיָ אֱלֹהֵינוּ, מֶלֶךְ הָעוֹלָם, אֲשֶׁר קִדְּשָׁנוּ
בְּמִצְוֹתָיו וְצִוָּנוּ לִקְבֹּעַ מְזוּזָה.

• • • • • • • • •

The first ten words of a בְּרָכָה שֶׁל מִצְוָה are always the same, but the ending changes according to the mitzvah you are about to perform.

Circle the endings of the three blessings above.

Which of these blessings is said when we put up a mezuzah on our doorpost?

Write the number: _____

52

Did You Know?

When we finish saying a blessing, the people around us respond with "Amen."
What does "Amen" mean?
Amen comes from the root אמן which means "to be firm," "to hold fast."
(אֱמוּנָה, *faith*, comes from the same root.) When we say Amen, we are showing
that we agree with the person who is saying the blessing. We are expressing our
faith in God.

● ● ● ● ● ● ● ● ●

The Holiday Connection

Read the following בְּרָכוֹת aloud.
On what holiday do we say each of the following blessings?
(The last word of each blessing is the clue word.)

Holiday	Blessing
	1 בָּרוּךְ אַתָּה, יְיָ אֱלֹהֵינוּ, מֶלֶךְ הָעוֹלָם, אֲשֶׁר קִדְּשָׁנוּ בְּמִצְוֹתָיו וְצִוָּנוּ לִשְׁמוֹעַ קוֹל שׁוֹפָר.
	2 בָּרוּךְ אַתָּה, יְיָ אֱלֹהֵינוּ, מֶלֶךְ הָעוֹלָם, אֲשֶׁר קִדְּשָׁנוּ בְּמִצְוֹתָיו וְצִוָּנוּ לֵישֵׁב בַּסֻּכָּה.
	3 בָּרוּךְ אַתָּה, יְיָ אֱלֹהֵינוּ, מֶלֶךְ הָעוֹלָם, אֲשֶׁר קִדְּשָׁנוּ בְּמִצְוֹתָיו וְצִוָּנוּ עַל מִקְרָא מְגִלָּה.
	4 בָּרוּךְ אַתָּה, יְיָ אֱלֹהֵינוּ, מֶלֶךְ הָעוֹלָם, אֲשֶׁר קִדְּשָׁנוּ בְּמִצְוֹתָיו וְצִוָּנוּ עַל אֲכִילַת מַצָּה.

Prayer Building Blocks

קִדְּשָׁנוּ "makes us holy"

....

קִדְּשָׁנוּ   means "makes us holy."

קִדְּשָׁנוּ   is made up of two parts:

קִדֵּשׁ   means "makes holy."

נוּ   means "us" or "our."

● ● ● ● ● ● ● ● ●

Add the ending that means "us" to complete this word:

קִדֵּשׁ _____

makes us holy

קִדְּשָׁנוּ is built on the root _____ _____ _____.

This root means _____.

Write the three root letters in the blanks to complete the word.

נוּ _____ _____ _____

makes us holy

54

בְּמִצְוֹתָיו "with God's commandments"

בְּמִצְוֹתָיו	means "with God's commandments."
בְּמִצְוֹתָיו	is made up of three parts:
בְּ	at the beginning of a word means "with" or "in."
מִצְוֹת	means "commandments."
ָיו	at the end of a word means "his."

As God is neither male nor female, we translate the word בְּמִצְוֹתָיו as *with God's commandments.*

• • • • • • • • •

Write the Hebrew word for "with God's commandments." _____

Draw a star above the part of this Hebrew word that means "with."

Circle the Hebrew word below that means "commandments."

מַצָּה   מִצְוָה   מִצְוֹת

Write this word in the blanks below.

בְּ _____ ָיו

Fill in the missing Hebrew word below.

בָּרוּךְ אַתָּה, יְיָ אֱלֹהֵינוּ, מֶלֶךְ הָעוֹלָם,

אֲשֶׁר קִדְּשָׁנוּ _____

55

וְצִוָּנוּ "and commands us"

. . . .

> **וְצִוָּנוּ**   means "and commands us."
>
> **וְצִוָּנוּ**   is a word made up of three parts:
>
> **וְ**   means "and."
>
> **צִוָּ**   means "commands."
>
> **נוּ**   means "us."

• • • • • • • • •

Copy the Hebrew word that means "and commands us." _____

The letters **ו** and **צ** appear in both of the following words:

בְּמִצְוֹתָיו   **וְצִוָּנוּ**

with God's commandments   and commands us

Draw a circle around the letters **ו** and **צ** in the two words above.

The letters **ו** and **צ** let us know that "command" is part of a word's meaning.

Write these two letters to complete the following words.

נוּ _____ _____ וְ   "and commands us."

תָיו _____ _____ בְּמִ   "with God's commandments"

Sketch-a-Blessing

Read the following בְּרָכוֹת. Draw a picture illustrating the object in each בְּרָכָה.

בָּרוּךְ אַתָּה, יְיָ אֱלֹהֵינוּ, מֶלֶךְ הָעוֹלָם,
אֲשֶׁר קִדְּשָׁנוּ בְּמִצְוֹתָיו וְצִוָּנוּ
לְהַדְלִיק נֵר שֶׁל שַׁבָּת.

בָּרוּךְ אַתָּה, יְיָ אֱלֹהֵינוּ, מֶלֶךְ הָעוֹלָם,
אֲשֶׁר קִדְּשָׁנוּ בְּמִצְוֹתָיו וְצִוָּנוּ
עַל נְטִילַת יָדָיִם (wash hands).

בָּרוּךְ אַתָּה, יְיָ אֱלֹהֵינוּ, מֶלֶךְ הָעוֹלָם,
אֲשֶׁר קִדְּשָׁנוּ בְּמִצְוֹתָיו וְצִוָּנוּ
עַל אֲכִילַת מָרוֹר.

בָּרוּךְ אַתָּה, יְיָ אֱלֹהֵינוּ, מֶלֶךְ הָעוֹלָם,
אֲשֶׁר קִדְּשָׁנוּ בְּמִצְוֹתָיו וְצִוָּנוּ
לְהִתְעַטֵּף בַּצִּיצִת

(wrap ourselves in a fringed garment — tallit).

57

Look Alikes

Sometimes the letter *vav* looks like this וֹ.
It looks like the vowel sound "Oh" טוֹ בוֹ קוֹ.
However, וֹ says "VO" if it follows a letter that already has a vowel, as in עָו and צָו.

• • • • • • • • •

Read each sound aloud.

עָו צָו עַו עָו

צָו עַו צָו עָו

Practice reading the following words.

מִצְוֹת	רָצָה	עֵוֹנִי	מִצְוָה	רְצוֹנֶךָ	1
רָצוֹן	צוֹדֵק	מִצְוֹתַי	לִרְצוֹן	עֲוֹנָתִי	2
וְצִוָּנוּ	בְּמִצְוֹת	מִצְרַיִם	אַרְצוֹת	בְּמִצְוֹתָיו	3
עָוֹן	מַצּוֹת	צוֹפִיָּה	צוֹרֶךְ	מְצוֹרָע	4
בְּמִצְוֹתַי	מִצְוַת	עֲוֹנָה	צַוֶּה	מִצִּיּוֹן	5

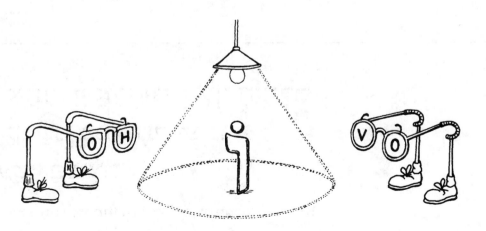

58

Fluent Reading

Each sentence contains a word you know. Practice reading the lines below.

• • • • • • • • •

1 בָּרוּךְ אַתָּה, יְיָ אֱלֹהֵינוּ, מֶלֶךְ הָעוֹלָם,

אֲשֶׁר קִדְּשָׁנוּ בְּמִצְוֹתָיו וְצִוָּנוּ לְהָנִיחַ תְּפִלִּין.

2 בָּרוּךְ אַתָּה, יְיָ, שׁוֹמֵעַ תְּפִלָּה.

3 בָּרוּךְ אַתָּה, יְיָ אֱלֹהֵינוּ, מֶלֶךְ הָעוֹלָם,

אֲשֶׁר קִדְּשָׁנוּ בְּמִצְוֹתָיו וְצִוָּנוּ עַל נְטִילַת לוּלָב.

4 בָּרוּךְ אַתָּה, יְיָ אֱלֹהֵינוּ, מֶלֶךְ הָעוֹלָם,

אֲשֶׁר קִדְּשָׁנוּ בְּמִצְוֹתָיו וְצִוָּנוּ עַל מִצְוַת תְּפִלִּין.

5 בָּרוּךְ אַתָּה, יְיָ אֱלֹהֵינוּ, מֶלֶךְ הָעוֹלָם,

אֲשֶׁר בִּדְבָרוֹ מַעֲרִיב עֲרָבִים.

6 בָּרוּךְ אַתָּה, יְיָ אֱלֹהֵינוּ, מֶלֶךְ הָעוֹלָם,

אֲשֶׁר נָתַן לָנוּ תּוֹרַת אֱמֶת.

7 בָּרוּךְ אַתָּה, יְיָ אֱלֹהֵינוּ, מֶלֶךְ הָעוֹלָם,

אֲשֶׁר קִדְּשָׁנוּ בְּמִצְוֹתָיו וְצִוָּנוּ לַעֲסוֹק בְּדִבְרֵי תוֹרָה.

7

It is Friday night. The family gathers together at home to welcome Shabbat. On the table is a fresh cloth, shiny dishes, and delicious food. On the table are also three important symbols of Shabbat — candles, wine, and ḥallah. We say a blessing over each one.

• • • • • • • • •

Practice reading the בְּרָכוֹת aloud.

1 בָּרוּךְ אַתָּה, יְיָ אֱלֹהֵינוּ, מֶלֶךְ הָעוֹלָם, אֲשֶׁר קִדְּשָׁנוּ
בְּמִצְוֹתָיו וְצִוָּנוּ לְהַדְלִיק נֵר שֶׁל שַׁבָּת.

Praised are You, Adonai our God, Ruler of the world, who makes us holy with commandments and commands us to light the Sabbath lights.

2 בָּרוּךְ אַתָּה, יְיָ אֱלֹהֵינוּ, מֶלֶךְ הָעוֹלָם, בּוֹרֵא פְּרִי הַגָּפֶן.

Praised are You, Adonai our God, Ruler of the world, who creates the fruit of the vine.

3 בָּרוּךְ אַתָּה, יְיָ אֱלֹהֵינוּ, מֶלֶךְ הָעוֹלָם, הַמּוֹצִיא לֶחֶם
מִן הָאָרֶץ.

Praised are You, Adonai our God, Ruler of the world, who brings forth bread from the earth.

Name the Shabbat Object

Complete each sentence by writing the word or drawing a picture.

Blessing #1 is said over the _____.

Blessing #2 is said over the _____.

Blessing #3 is said over the _____.

לְהַדְלִיק

to light

נֵר

a light, candle

שֶׁל

of

שַׁבָּת

Shabbat

Lighting the Candles

Every Friday evening as the sun goes down, we light candles to welcome Shabbat with joy, and we say the blessing over the candles. The flames cast a peaceful glow on our dinner table. Shabbat has begun!

• • • • • • • • •

Match Game

Connect the Hebrew word to its English meaning.

ruler	בָּרוּךְ
to light	שַׁבָּת
light, candle	מֶלֶךְ
Shabbat	נֵר
praised	לְהַדְלִיק

61

Unscramble the Prayer

Write the ending of the candle blessing in the correct order.

בָּרוּךְ אַתָּה, יְיָ אֱלֹהֵינוּ, מֶלֶךְ הָעוֹלָם,
אֲשֶׁר קִדְּשָׁנוּ בְּמִצְוֹתָיו וְצִוָּנוּ...

שַׁבָּת   לְהַדְלִיק   שֶׁל   נֵר

_____

• • • • • • • • •

Did You Know?

Do you know why we light *two* candles on Shabbat?

The Ten Commandments appear twice in the Torah.

The first time — in the Book of Exodus — Adonai tells us to "*Remember* the Shabbat."

The second time — in the Book of Deuteronomy — Adonai tells us to "*Observe* the Shabbat."

The two candles remind us of both these commandments.

But many people light more than two candles. In some homes candles are lit for every member of the family. There is no limit to the number of candles you can light.

Candles and Light

Candles and light play an important role in Judaism. The Ḥanukkah candles flicker and glow on your window ledge. We light a Yahrzeit candle to remember the anniversary of a loved one's death. And the Eternal Light burns above the Holy Ark.

• • • • • • • • •

Practice reading each of these blessings recited over candles.

1 בָּרוּךְ אַתָּה, יְיָ אֱלֹהֵינוּ, מֶלֶךְ הָעוֹלָם, אֲשֶׁר קִדְּשָׁנוּ
בְּמִצְוֹתָיו וְצִוָּנוּ לְהַדְלִיק נֵר שֶׁל שַׁבָּת.

2 בָּרוּךְ אַתָּה, יְיָ אֱלֹהֵינוּ, מֶלֶךְ הָעוֹלָם, אֲשֶׁר קִדְּשָׁנוּ
בְּמִצְוֹתָיו וְצִוָּנוּ לְהַדְלִיק נֵר שֶׁל יוֹם טוֹב.

3 בָּרוּךְ אַתָּה, יְיָ אֱלֹהֵינוּ, מֶלֶךְ הָעוֹלָם, אֲשֶׁר קִדְּשָׁנוּ
בְּמִצְוֹתָיו וְצִוָּנוּ לְהַדְלִיק נֵר שֶׁל (שַׁבָּת וְשֶׁל) יוֹם טוֹב.

4 בָּרוּךְ אַתָּה, יְיָ אֱלֹהֵינוּ, מֶלֶךְ הָעוֹלָם, אֲשֶׁר קִדְּשָׁנוּ
בְּמִצְוֹתָיו וְצִוָּנוּ לְהַדְלִיק נֵר שֶׁל חֲנֻכָּה.

5 בָּרוּךְ אַתָּה, יְיָ אֱלֹהֵינוּ, מֶלֶךְ הָעוֹלָם,
בּוֹרֵא מְאוֹרֵי הָאֵשׁ.

Food for Thought

A blessing is usually said *before* the action takes place. For example, when we eat an apple, first we say the בְּרָכָה (...בּוֹרֵא פְּרִי הָעֵץ) and then take the first bite.

But in the case of the Shabbat candles, we light the candles *first* and say the blessing *afterwards*.

Why?

Once we say the blessing, Shabbat begins. Many people will not light a match on Shabbat. Therefore, we light the match (and the candles) *first* and say the blessing *afterwards*.

• • • • • • • • •

PRAYER DICTIONARY

בּוֹרֵא

who creates

_____

פְּרִי

(the) fruit (of)

_____

הַגֶּפֶן

the vine

Blessing for the Wine

The Shabbat meal would not be complete without wine. The Bible tells us that wine adds joy to life. Wine helps make Shabbat special and holy.

We say a בְּרָכָה over the wine to thank יְיָ for making the grapes grow. We may pick the grapes and turn them into wine, but it is יְיָ who ensures that the vine produces its fruit.

Complete the following activities for the blessing of the wine.

בָּרוּךְ אַתָּה, יְיָ אֱלֹהֵינוּ, מֶלֶךְ הָעוֹלָם,
בּוֹרֵא פְּרִי הַגָּפֶן.

• • • • • • • • •

1. Circle the word that means "fruit."

2. Draw a box around the Hebrew word that means "who creates."

3. Underline the word for "praised."

4. Write the English meaning of מֶלֶךְ. _____

5. Put a ✡ over the word for "the vine."

6. Write the part of הָעוֹלָם that means "the." _____

7. Write the part of הַגֶּפֶן that means "the." _____

8. What is another English word for "the fruit of the vine"?

_____

65

Blessing for the Bread

The bread we eat on Shabbat is called ḥallah (חַלָה). Ḥallot come in different shapes and sizes, some have seeds or raisins, some are plain.

But no matter what bread we eat, we do not take it for granted.

We say a blessing — הַמּוֹצִיא — to show that every meal is special. We feel lucky to have food to eat. We thank יְיָ for giving us this food.

Practice reading הַמּוֹצִיא.

בָּרוּךְ אַתָּה, יְיָ אֱלֹהֵינוּ, מֶלֶךְ הָעוֹלָם, 1
הַמּוֹצִיא לֶחֶם מִן הָאָרֶץ. 2

66

הַמּוֹצִיא

who brings forth

לֶחֶם

bread

מִן

from

הָאָרֶץ

the earth

Word Match

Match the English word to its Hebrew meaning.

A. who creates

B. the world

C. fruit

D. the vine

E. from

F. the earth

G. bread

( ) מִן

( ) פְּרִי

( ) הָאָרֶץ

( ) בּוֹרֵא

( ) הַגֶּפֶן

( ) הָעוֹלָם

( ) לֶחֶם

• • • • • • • • •

Did You Know?

Bread is the most important food in Jewish life.

In the Bible there are many examples of guests being offered bread to eat. Abraham and Sarah, who are famous for their hospitality, immediately served bread to make their guests feel welcome.

In fact, bread is so important that one blessing said at the beginning of a meal — הַמּוֹצִיא — covers all the food to be eaten during that meal.

Unscramble the Prayer

Write the ending of the בְּרָכָה in the correct order.

בָּרוּךְ אַתָּה, יְיָ אֱלֹהֵינוּ, מֶלֶךְ הָעוֹלָם...

מִן הַמּוֹצִיא הָאָרֶץ לֶחֶם

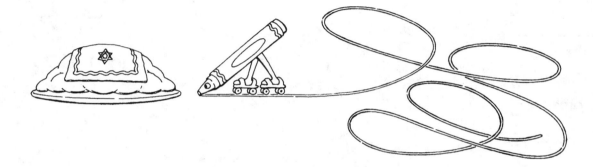

The Holiday Connection

As we begin to tell the Passover story at our seder, we uncover a plate of matzah and lift it up for all at the table to see. As we recall that our ancestors ate this "bread of affliction" when they were slaves in Egypt, we announce: "Let all who are hungry come and eat."

• • • • • • • • •

A Point To Ponder

Why is the mitzvah of *Feeding the Hungry* (מַאֲכִיל רְעֵבִים) so closely linked to our lives in Egypt?

68

An Ethical Echo

In the Book of Deuteronomy there is a passage that says "You too must befriend the stranger, for you were strangers in the Land of Egypt." What better way is there to welcome a stranger than to open your home to him or her! The mitzvah of *Hospitality* (הַכְנָסַת אוֹרְחִים) is made greater when you offer your guest food and drink.

A Point to Ponder

A new student joins your class in the middle of the school year. What can you do to befriend this stranger?

Why is the experience of our ancestors in Egypt more than 3,000 years ago still relevant today?

• • • • • • • • •

69

Birkat HaMazon

Not only do we thank יְיָ for the food *before* we eat it, we also thank יְיָ upon completion of the meal.

We say Grace After Meals (in Hebrew, בִּרְכַּת הַמָּזוֹן).

• • • • • • • • •

Practice reading this section of בִּרְכַּת הַמָּזוֹן.

1   בָּרוּךְ אַתָּה, יְיָ אֱלֹהֵינוּ, מֶלֶךְ הָעוֹלָם,

2   הַזָּן אֶת הָעוֹלָם כֻּלוֹ בְּטוּבוֹ,

3   בְּחֵן בְּחֶסֶד וּבְרַחֲמִים.

4   הוּא נוֹתֵן לֶחֶם לְכָל בָּשָׂר, כִּי לְעוֹלָם חַסְדּוֹ.

5   וּבְטוּבוֹ הַגָּדוֹל תָּמִיד לֹא חָסַר לָנוּ,

6   וְאַל יֶחְסַר לָנוּ מָזוֹן לְעוֹלָם וָעֶד. בַּעֲבוּר שְׁמוֹ הַגָּדוֹל

7   כִּי הוּא אֵל זָן וּמְפַרְנֵס לַכֹּל,

8   וּמֵטִיב לַכֹּל, וּמֵכִין מָזוֹן לְכָל בְּרִיּוֹתָיו אֲשֶׁר בָּרָא.

9   בָּרוּךְ אַתָּה יְיָ, הַזָּן אֶת הַכֹּל.

• • • • • • • • •

Did You Know?

The full בִּרְכַּת הַמָּזוֹן is said only after a meal at which bread has been consumed.

You can see how important bread really is.

Fluent Reading

Each phrase contains a word you know. Practice reading the lines below.

• • • • • • • • •

1 וְשַׁבַּת קׇדְשׁוֹ בְּאַהֲבָה וּבְרָצוֹן הִנְחִילָנוּ.

2 וְשָׁמְרוּ בְנֵי יִשְׂרָאֵל אֶת הַשַּׁבָּת,
   לַעֲשׂוֹת אֶת הַשַּׁבָּת לְדֹרֹתָם.

3 בָּרוּךְ אַתָּה, יְיָ אֱלֹהֵינוּ, מֶלֶךְ הָעוֹלָם,
   עֹשֶׂה מַעֲשֵׂה בְרֵאשִׁית.

4 בְּרֵאשִׁית בָּרָא אֱלֹהִים אֵת הַשָּׁמַיִם וְאֵת הָאָרֶץ.

5 אֲדוֹן הַשָּׁלוֹם, מְקַדֵּשׁ הַשַּׁבָּת וּמְבָרֵךְ שְׁבִיעִי.

6 בָּרוּךְ אַתָּה יְיָ, מֶלֶךְ עַל כָּל הָאָרֶץ,
   מְקַדֵּשׁ יִשְׂרָאֵל וְיוֹם הַזִּכָּרוֹן.

7 זִכָּרוֹן לְמַעֲשֵׂה בְרֵאשִׁית.

8 טוֹבִים מְאוֹרוֹת שֶׁבָּרָא אֱלֹהֵינוּ.

9 בָּרוּךְ אַתָּה, יְיָ אֱלֹהֵינוּ, מֶלֶךְ הָעוֹלָם,
   אֲשֶׁר קִדְּשָׁנוּ בְּמִצְוֹתָיו וְצִוָּנוּ לְהַדְלִיק נֵר שֶׁל שַׁבָּת.

8   קִדּוּשׁ

Every Friday evening, before we say הַמּוֹצִיא and begin the meal, we say a special prayer called קִדּוּשׁ (Kiddush). Kiddush means *sanctification* or *making holy*. Kiddush helps make Shabbat holy.

● ● ● ● ● ● ● ● ●

The קִדּוּשׁ begins with a בְּרָכָה you have already learned.

בָּרוּךְ אַתָּה, יְיָ אֱלֹהֵינוּ, מֶלֶךְ הָעוֹלָם, בּוֹרֵא פְּרִי הַגָּפֶן.

Can you say this בְּרָכָה by heart?

Practice reading the קִדּוּשׁ aloud.

1. בָּרוּךְ אַתָּה, יְיָ אֱלֹהֵינוּ, מֶלֶךְ הָעוֹלָם, בּוֹרֵא פְּרִי הַגָּפֶן.
2. בָּרוּךְ אַתָּה, יְיָ אֱלֹהֵינוּ, מֶלֶךְ הָעוֹלָם, אֲשֶׁר קִדְּשָׁנוּ
3. בְּמִצְוֹתָיו וְרָצָה בָנוּ, וְשַׁבַּת קָדְשׁוֹ בְּאַהֲבָה וּבְרָצוֹן
4. הִנְחִילָנוּ, זִכָּרוֹן לְמַעֲשֵׂה בְרֵאשִׁית. כִּי הוּא יוֹם תְּחִלָּה
5. לְמִקְרָאֵי קֹדֶשׁ, זֵכֶר לִיצִיאַת מִצְרָיִם. כִּי בָנוּ בָחַרְתָּ
6. וְאוֹתָנוּ קִדַּשְׁתָּ מִכָּל הָעַמִּים, וְשַׁבַּת קָדְשְׁךָ בְּאַהֲבָה
7. וּבְרָצוֹן הִנְחַלְתָּנוּ. בָּרוּךְ אַתָּה יְיָ, מְקַדֵּשׁ הַשַּׁבָּת.

*Praised are You, Adonai our God, Ruler of the world, who creates the fruit of the vine.
Praised are You, Adonai our God, Ruler of the world, who makes us holy with commandments and takes delight in us. In God's love and favor God has made the holy Sabbath our heritage, as a memory of the work of creation.
It is first among our holy days, a memory of the going out from Egypt.
You chose us from all the nations and You made us holy, and in love and favor You have given us the Sabbath as a sacred inheritance.
Praised are You, Adonai, who makes the Sabbath holy.*

Word Check

Put a ✔ next to the Hebrew word that means the same as the English.

קִדּוּשׁ

sanctification

זִכָּרוֹן

memory

(לְ)מַעֲשֵׂה בְּרֵאשִׁית

the work of creation

זֵכֶר

memory

(לִ)יצִיאַת מִצְרַיִם

the going out from Egypt

1   □ אַהֲבָה   memory
   □ זִכָּרוֹן

2   □ לְעוֹלָם וָעֶד   the going out from Egypt
   □ יְצִיאַת מִצְרַיִם

3   □ זֵכֶר   memory
   □ מִצְרַיִם

4   □ קִדּוּשׁ   sanctification
   □ בָּרוּךְ

5   □ נֵר שֶׁל שַׁבָּת   the work of creation
   □ מַעֲשֵׂה בְּרֵאשִׁית

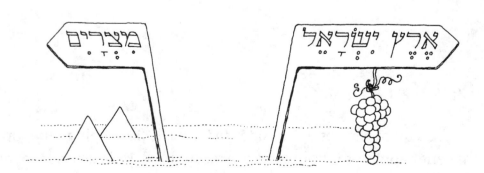

What's Missing?

Complete each phrase with the missing word.

1 זִכָּרוֹן לְמַעֲשֵׂה בְרֵאשִׁית   a memory of the work of _____

2 זֵכֶר לִיצִיאַת מִצְרָיִם   a memory of the going out from _____

3 בָּרוּךְ אַתָּה, יְיָ   Praised are You _____

4 אֱלֹהֵינוּ, מֶלֶךְ הָעוֹלָם   our God, Ruler of _____

• • • • • • • • •

Did You Know?

The cup of wine used for Kiddush is usually filled right to the top. This is to show that our happiness is brimming over as we bless יְיָ. We hope that our lives will overflow with good things.

Prayer Building Blocks

קִדּוּשׁ "sanctification"

קִדּוּשׁ   means "sanctification" (making holy).

קִדּוּשׁ   makes שַׁבָּת holy.

We know that the root letters קדש mean "holy."

• • • • • • • • •

The following words all appear in the Kiddush. Read them aloud.
Circle the three root letters in each word.

קִדְּשָׁנוּ   קָדְשׁוֹ   קֹדֶשׁ   קִדַּשְׁתָּ   קָדְשְׁךָ   מְקַדֵּשׁ

Read the following lines, and circle the words built on the root קדש.

1. וְשַׁבַּת קָדְשׁוֹ בְּאַהֲבָה וּבְרָצוֹן הִנְחִילָנוּ

2. נְקַדֵּשׁ אֶת שִׁמְךָ בָּעוֹלָם כְּשֵׁם שֶׁמַּקְדִּישִׁים אוֹתוֹ

3. וַיְבָרֶךְ אֱלֹהִים אֶת יוֹם הַשְּׁבִיעִי וַיְקַדֵּשׁ אֹתוֹ

4. קָדוֹשׁ קָדוֹשׁ קָדוֹשׁ יְיָ צְבָאוֹת

5. אַתָּה קִדַּשְׁתָּ אֶת יוֹם הַשְּׁבִיעִי לִשְׁמֶךָ

זִכָּרוֹן, זֵכֶר "memory"

The קָדוּשׁ recited on שַׁבָּת helps us *remember* why we celebrate שַׁבָּת and make it holy.

The letters זכר tell us that "remember" is part of a word's meaning.

זִכָּרוֹן   means "memory."

זֵכֶר   also means "memory."

● ● ● ● ● ● ● ● ●

What three letters are in both זִכָּרוֹן and זֵכֶר? _____ _____ _____.

Complete the following words by writing the three Hebrew letters that tell us "remember" is part of the word's meaning.

וֹן _____ _____ _____   means "memory."

_____ _____ _____   means "memory."

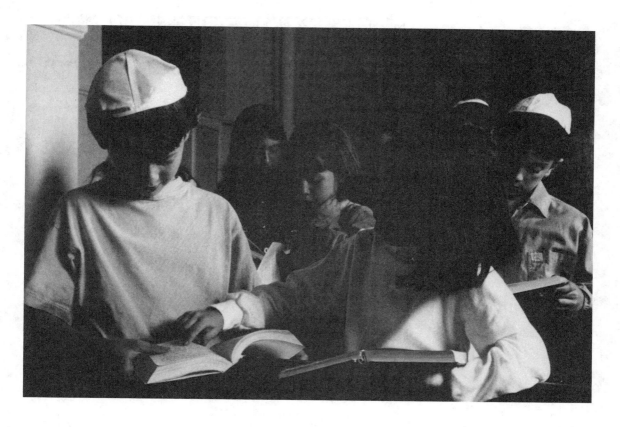

76

The קִדוּשׁ helps us remember events in our history that are reasons for joy. One reason for joy is mentioned in these words from the קִדוּשׁ prayer.

$$\text{זִכָּרוֹן לְמַעֲשֵׂה בְרֵאשִׁית}$$

memory of the work of creation

Circle the Hebrew word that means "memory."

Another reason for joy is found in the following words from the קִדוּשׁ prayer.

$$\text{זֵכֶר לִיצִיאַת מִצְרָיִם}$$

memory of the going out from Egypt

Circle the Hebrew word that means "memory."

Which three letters tell us that "remember" is part of a word's meaning?

_____ _____ _____

Read the following sentences and circle the words built on the root זכר.

1. וַיֹּאמֶר מֹשֶׁה אֶל הָעָם, זָכוֹר אֶת הַיּוֹם הַזֶּה.

2. בָּרוּךְ אַתָּה, יְיָ אֱלֹהֵינוּ, מֶלֶךְ הָעוֹלָם, זוֹכֵר הַבְּרִית,

   וְנֶאֱמָן בִּבְרִיתוֹ וְקַיָּם בְּמַאֲמָרוֹ.

3. מְקַדֵּשׁ יִשְׂרָאֵל וְיוֹם הַזִּכָּרוֹן.

4. לְמַעַן תִּזְכְּרוּ וַעֲשִׂיתֶם אֶת כָּל מִצְוֹתַי, וִהְיִיתֶם קְדֹשִׁים

   לֵאלֹהֵיכֶם.

5. וּזְכַרְתֶּם אֶת כָּל מִצְוֹת יְיָ וַעֲשִׂיתֶם אֹתָם.

The Holiday Connection

There is a special day in the Jewish year when we remember all the brave soldiers who died in Israel's wars. We call this day יוֹם הַזִּכָּרוֹן, the Day of Remembrance. יוֹם הַזִּכָּרוֹן is celebrated in Israel on the day before יוֹם הָעַצְמָאוּת, Israel's Independence Day.

● ● ● ● ● ● ● ● ●

Why do you think the solemn יוֹם הַזִּכָּרוֹן is observed one day before the joyous Day of Independence?

_____

_____

_____

לְ(מַעֲשֵׂה בְּרֵאשִׁית (לְ "work of creation"

When we say קִדּוּשׁ we remember two important events. One of them is the creation of the world.

מַעֲשֵׂה   means "work of."

בְּרֵאשִׁית   means "creation" (in the beginning).

בְּרֵאשִׁית   is also the Hebrew name for Genesis, the
first book of the תּוֹרָה.

• • • • • • • • •

Which of the following is not a meaning of בְּרֵאשִׁית? Circle it.

      creation   Torah   Genesis   in the beginning

Draw a circle around the Hebrew word that means "the work of."

זִכָּרוֹן לְמַעֲשֵׂה בְּרֵאשִׁית

Now draw a star above the Hebrew word that means "creation."

Write the phrase in the correct order.

בְּרֵאשִׁית   לְמַעֲשֵׂה   זִכָּרוֹן

_____ _____ _____

(לְ)יְצִיאַת מִצְרַיִם "going out from Egypt"

The second important event we remember in the קִדּוּשׁ is the *going out from Egypt.*

יְצִיאַת means "going out from."

מִצְרַיִם means "Egypt."

• • • • • • • • •

Draw a circle around the Hebrew word that means "going out from."

זֵכֶר לִיצִיאַת מִצְרַיִם

Now draw a star above the Hebrew word that means "Egypt."

Write the phrase in the correct order.

מִצְרַיִם לִיצִיאַת זֵכֶר

_____ _____ _____

What's Missing?

Use the words below to complete the sentences.

Shabbat   Adonai   six   Kiddush   seventh

We mention Creation in the _____ prayer because we remember

that _____ created the world in _____ days and rested

on the _____ day. We call that day _____ .

80

Name the Picture

Choose and circle the Hebrew word or phrase that best identifies each picture below.

בּוֹרֵא פְּרִי הַגֶּפֶן
לְהַדְלִיק נֵר
הַמּוֹצִיא לֶחֶם

בָּרוּךְ
קָדוֹשׁ
הַשַּׁבָּת

בְּרֵאשִׁית
לְמַעֲשֶׂה
שְׁמוֹת

זֵכֶר/זִכָּרוֹן
לְמַעֲשֶׂה
בְּרֵאשִׁית

זֵכֶר
לִיצִיאַת
מִצְרָיִם

זֵכֶר
לִיצִיאַת
מִצְרָיִם

Kiddush Quiz

בָּרוּךְ אַתָּה, יְיָ אֱלֹהֵינוּ, מֶלֶךְ הָעוֹלָם, בּוֹרֵא פְּרִי הַגָּפֶן. 1

בָּרוּךְ אַתָּה, יְיָ אֱלֹהֵינוּ, מֶלֶךְ הָעוֹלָם, אֲשֶׁר קִדְּשָׁנוּ 2

בְּמִצְוֹתָיו וְרָצָה בָנוּ, וְשַׁבַּת קָדְשׁוֹ בְּאַהֲבָה וּבְרָצוֹן 3

הִנְחִילָנוּ, זִכָּרוֹן לְמַעֲשֵׂה בְרֵאשִׁית. כִּי הוּא יוֹם תְּחִלָּה 4

לְמִקְרָאֵי קֹדֶשׁ, זֵכֶר לִיצִיאַת מִצְרָיִם. כִּי בָנוּ בָחַרְתָּ 5

וְאוֹתָנוּ קִדַּשְׁתָּ מִכָּל הָעַמִּים, וְשַׁבַּת קָדְשְׁךָ בְּאַהֲבָה 6

וּבְרָצוֹן הִנְחַלְתָּנוּ. בָּרוּךְ אַתָּה יְיָ, מְקַדֵּשׁ הַשַּׁבָּת. 7

Complete these questions on the קִדּוּשׁ.

1. How many different בְּרָכוֹת can you find in the קִדּוּשׁ? _____

2. What are the clue words when looking for a בְּרָכָה? Write them here.

_____

3. קִדּוּשׁ is built on the root קדשׁ. The root קדשׁ means _____.
In the prayer there are many Hebrew words based on the root קדשׁ.
Circle every word that has this root. Can you read all the circled words fluently?

4. In the קִדּוּשׁ we recall two important events.

What are they?   1. _____

2. _____

5. Circle the three root letters in these words.

זְכָרוֹן   זֵכֶר

Write the root here. _____ _____ _____ What does this root mean?

82

Fluent Reading

Each phrase contains a word you know. Practice reading the lines below.

● ● ● ● ● ● ● ● ●

1 חֶמְדַּת יָמִים אוֹתוֹ קָרָאתָ, זֵכֶר לְמַעֲשֵׂה בְרֵאשִׁית.

2 בָּרוּךְ אַתָּה, יְיָ אֱלֹהֵינוּ, מֶלֶךְ הָעוֹלָם,
   עֹשֶׂה מַעֲשֵׂה בְרֵאשִׁית.

3 אִלּוּ הוֹצִיאָנוּ מִמִּצְרַיִם וְלֹא קָרַע לָנוּ אֶת הַיָּם – דַּיֵּנוּ!

4 בָּרוּךְ אַתָּה, יְיָ, מְקַדֵּשׁ הַשַּׁבָּת וְיִשְׂרָאֵל וְהַזְּמַנִּים.

5 בָּרוּךְ שֶׁנָּתַן תּוֹרָה לְעַמּוֹ יִשְׂרָאֵל בִּקְדֻשָּׁתוֹ.

6 עֲבָדִים הָיִינוּ לְפַרְעֹה בְּמִצְרָיִם.

7 זָכוֹר אֶת יוֹם הַשַּׁבָּת לְקַדְּשׁוֹ.

8 מִצְוָה עָלֵינוּ לְסַפֵּר בִּיצִיאַת מִצְרָיִם.

9 וְאָהַבְתָּ לוֹ כָּמוֹךָ, כִּי גֵרִים הֱיִיתֶם בְּאֶרֶץ מִצְרָיִם.

83

9   קִדּוּשׁ

The Jews have a special relationship with God. The Torah tells us that the Jews were chosen by God, not for special privileges, but for special duties and responsibilities. The Jews are sometimes called the "treasured people" or the "chosen people" in the Bible and in the Siddur.

The Jews have a big responsibility: to follow the laws of the Torah and to be good, decent people.

In the קִדּוּשׁ we speak about God choosing us from among the nations and making us a holy people.

• • • • • • • • •

Word Check

Put a ✔ next to the correct English meaning.

וְאוֹתָנוּ קִדַּשְׁתָּ   and You made us holy   ☐

                                          and You helped us   ☐

בְּאַהֲבָה   in glory   ☐

                         in love   ☐

בָּנוּ בָחַרְתָּ   You blessed us   ☐

                         You chose us   ☐

מִכָּל הָעַמִּים   from all the nations   ☐

                         forever and ever   ☐

וּבְרָצוֹן   and in favor   ☐

                         and in hope   ☐

Fill in the Blanks

Write the English phrase above its Hebrew meaning.

_____	_____	_____
בָּנוּ בָחַרְתָּ	בְּאַהֲבָה	וּבְרָצוֹן

_____	_____
מִכָּל הָעַמִּים	וְאוֹתָנוּ קִדַּשְׁתָּ

Prayer Dictionary (side column):

בְּאַהֲבָה
in love

וּבְרָצוֹן
and in favor

בָּנוּ
us

בָחַרְתָּ
You chose

וְאוֹתָנוּ קִדַּשְׁתָּ
and You made us holy

מִכָּל הָעַמִּים
from all the nations

Understanding the Prayer

Read these words and complete the activities listed below.

בְּאַהֲבָה וּבְרָצוֹן... בָּנוּ בָחַרְתָּ וְאוֹתָנוּ קִדַּשְׁתָּ מִכָּל הָעַמִּים

1. Draw a triangle above the phrase that means "from all the nations."
2. Circle the phrase that means "You chose us."
3. Draw a ❤ above the word that means "in love."
4. Draw a ✡ above the phrase that means "and You made us holy."
5. Underline twice the word that means "and in favor."

• • • • • • • • •

Did You Know?

The leader of the service recites the קִדּוּשׁ at the end of Friday evening services *and* we say the קִדּוּשׁ at home before our Shabbat meal.

Why is the קִדּוּשׁ said *twice* on a Friday evening?

The custom of saying the קִדּוּשׁ both at home and in the synagogue began almost 2,000 years ago. Travelers who were far from their homes were often fed and sheltered in the synagogue. To ensure that these people heard the קִדּוּשׁ the leader of the service recited it in the synagogue for all to hear.

Another reason the קִדּוּשׁ is recited in the synagogue is that wine has always been considered a luxury, which some people cannot afford in their homes. One glass of wine in the synagogue allows all the people there to fulfill the mitzvah of saying the קִדּוּשׁ.

Prayer Building Blocks

בְּאַהֲבָה "in love"

....

בְּאַהֲבָה	means "in love."
בְּאַהֲבָה	is made up of two parts:
בְּ	at the beginning of a word means "in" or "with."
אַהֲבָה	means "love."

• • • • • • • • •

Write the Hebrew word that means "in love." _____

Circle the prefix that means "in" in the following Hebrew word.

בְּאַהֲבָה

To the following prefix, add the Hebrew word meaning "love."

בְּ_____

What does this Hebrew word mean in English? _____

87

וּבְרָצוֹן "and in favor"

וּבְרָצוֹן	means "and in favor."
וּבְרָצוֹן	is made up of three parts:
וּ	means "and."
בְּ	at the beginning of a word means "in."
רָצוֹן	means "favor."

• • • • • • • • •

Write the Hebrew word that means "and in favor." _____

To the following prefix, add the Hebrew word meaning "favor."

וּבְ _____

Circle the prefix that means "and" in the following Hebrew word.

וּבְרָצוֹן

Fill in the missing English words below.

וְשַׁבַּת קָדְשׁוֹ בְּאַהֲבָה וּבְרָצוֹן

And God's holy Sabbath, in love _____

וְאוֹתָנוּ קִדַּשְׁתָּ "and You made us holy"

וְאוֹתָנוּ   means "and us."

קִדַּשְׁתָּ   means "You made holy."

● ● ● ● ● ● ● ● ●

Write the Hebrew word that means "You made holy." _____

The following words all have to do with "holy." Circle the three letters that appear in all the words and that let us know "holy" is part of the word's meaning.

קִדַּשְׁתָּ   קִדְּשָׁנוּ   קָדוֹשׁ

Write the missing Hebrew word that means "You made holy."

כִּי בָנוּ בָחַרְתָּ וְאוֹתָנוּ _____ .

Because You chose us and <u>You made</u> us <u>holy</u>.

89

So far we know that קִדַּשְׁתָּ means "You (God) made holy." But whom or what did God make holy? God made us— אוֹתָנוּ —holy.

● ● ● ● ● ● ● ● ●

Write the Hebrew word that tells whom God made holy. _____

The Hebrew words אוֹתָנוּ and בָנוּ both mean _____ in English.

Circle the ending that means "us" in the two Hebrew words above.

Fill in the missing Hebrew word that tells us whom God made holy.

כִּי בָנוּ בָחַרְתָּ וְ _____ קִדַּשְׁתָּ.

Because You chose us and You made <u>us</u> holy.

Circle the Hebrew word that means "You made holy."

כִּי בָנוּ בָחַרְתָּ וְאוֹתָנוּ קִדַּשְׁתָּ.

Because You chose us and <u>You made</u> us <u>holy</u>.

Find the two Hebrew words that mean "us," and write them below.

_____ _____

Holiness in You and Me

The Jews are members of a "holy nation." Each and every one of us has the potential to be holy. Fulfilling mitzvot can add holiness to our lives. What do you think "being holy" means?

Put a ✔ next to the ways we can add holiness to our lives.

___ lighting Shabbat candles

___ watching a golden sunset

___ studying the Torah

___ watching television

___ baking brownies for a sick friend

Can you add one more example of your own?

_____

מִכָּל הָעַמִּים "from all the nations"

מִכָּל   means "from all."

הָעַמִּים   means "the nations."

• • • • • • • •

מִכָּל   is made up of two parts:

מִ   means "from."

כָּל   means "all."

Draw a circle around the part of the word below that means "from."

מִכָּל

Now draw a star above the part of the word that means "all."

Complete the following Hebrew phrase.

כִּי בָנוּ בָחַרְתָּ וְאוֹתָנוּ קִדַּשְׁתָּ _____ הָעַמִּים.

Because You chose us <u>from all</u> the nations and You made us holy.

• • • • • • • •

הָעַמִּים   means "the nations."

הָעַמִּים   is made up of two parts:

הָ   is a prefix meaning "the."

עַמִּים   means "nations."

Add the Hebrew word for "nations" to the prefix meaning "the."

הָ_____

עַמִּים means "nations."

עַם means "nation" or "people."

Another name for the Jews is the "people of Israel."

עַם יִשְׂרָאֵל

• • • • • • • • •

Write the Hebrew words that mean "people of Israel."

_____   _____

When we refer to more than one group of people, we use

עַמִּים

When we refer to only one group of people, we use

עַם

Write the Hebrew word meaning "nation" or "people" that refers to more than one group.

_____

Choose the correct Hebrew word to complete the sentence below.

עַם   אַתָּה   עַמִּים

כִּי בָנוּ בָחַרְתָּ וְאוֹתָנוּ קִדַשְׁתָּ מִכָּל הָ_____.

Because You chose us from all the <u>nations</u> and You made us holy.

The "Chosen" People

The Rabbis tell us that God offered the Torah to other peoples before offering it to יִשְׂרָאֵל. Each nation refused because they could not and would not follow the laws of the Torah.

When God offered the Torah to יִשְׂרָאֵל, they answered נַעֲשֶׂה וְנִשְׁמָע, "We shall do, and we shall obey."

● ● ● ● ● ● ● ● ●

Read this rhyme about "chosenness" and explain the last line in your own words.

How odd of God
To choose the Jews!
It's not that odd —
The Jews chose God!

_____

_____

Look Alikes

The letters כ and כ look alike but are pronounced differently. Each sentence below contains at least one of these letters. Practice reading the sentences below.

1. כָּל עוֹד בַּלֵּבָב פְּנִימָה נֶפֶשׁ יְהוּדִי הוֹמִיָּה.

2. בְּכָל עֵת וּבְכָל שָׁעָה בִּשְׁלוֹמֶךָ.

3. וּלְקַיֵּם אֶת כָּל דִּבְרֵי תַלְמוּד תּוֹרָתֶךָ בְּאַהֲבָה.

4. וְאָהַבְתָּ אֵת יְיָ אֱלֹהֶיךָ בְּכָל לְבָבְךָ וּבְכָל נַפְשְׁךָ

5. וּבְכָל מְאֹדֶךָ.

6. עֹשֶׂה שָׁלוֹם וּבוֹרֵא אֶת הַכֹּל.

7. וּבָנוּ בָחַרְתָּ מִכָּל עָם.

Fluent Reading

Each phrase contains a word you know. Practice reading the lines below.

● ● ● ● ● ● ● ● ●

1 וַיְכֻלּוּ הַשָּׁמַיִם וְהָאָרֶץ וְכָל צְבָאָם.

2 וַיְבָרֶךְ אֱלֹהִים אֶת יוֹם הַשְּׁבִיעִי וַיְקַדֵּשׁ אֹתוֹ.

3 וּמֵבִיא גּוֹאֵל לִבְנֵי בְנֵיהֶם, לְמַעַן שְׁמוֹ, בְּאַהֲבָה.

4 וּמַלְכוּתוֹ בְּרָצוֹן קִבְּלוּ עֲלֵיהֶם.

5 אַתָּה קִדַּשְׁתָּ אֶת יוֹם הַשְּׁבִיעִי לִשְׁמֶךָ.

6 לִבְנֵי יִשְׂרָאֵל עַם קְרֹבוֹ, הַלְלוּיָהּ!

7 זָכוֹר אֶת יוֹם הַשַּׁבָּת לְקַדְּשׁוֹ.

8 בָּרוּךְ אַתָּה, יְיָ, הַמְבָרֵךְ אֶת עַמּוֹ יִשְׂרָאֵל בַּשָּׁלוֹם.

9 בָּרוּךְ אַתָּה, יְיָ אֱלֹהֵינוּ, מֶלֶךְ הָעוֹלָם, אֲשֶׁר בָּחַר בָּנוּ
מִכָּל הָעַמִּים וְנָתַן לָנוּ אֶת תּוֹרָתוֹ.

You have learned some of our most important prayers and blessings. You can recite some of these prayers in the synagogue; others you and your family can say together as you share Shabbat dinners or when you celebrate Jewish holidays—lighting a ḥanukkiah, sitting in a sukkah, eating matzah on Passover. These prayers will help you to be an active participant in Jewish life.

But there's still much more to come.

In the next book you will learn the deep feelings we express in the *Amidah*, you will see how we show our love for Jewish learning in the Torah service, you will study the prayers that end the Shabbat Morning Service. And you will see how these prayers relate to *your* life as a Jew.

Congratulations on completing *Book 1*.

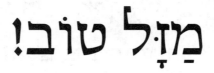

מַזָּל טוֹב!